Implementing NICE Guidance

A Practical Handbook for Professionals

National Prescribing Centre

Radcliffe Medical Press

© 2001 National Prescribing Centre

Radcliffe Medical Press Ltd
18 Marcham Road, Abingdon, Oxon OX14 1AA

British Library Cataloguing in Publication Data

A catalogue record for this book is available from the British Library.

ISBN 1 85775 524 3

Typeset by Aarontype Ltd, Easton, Bristol
Printed and Bound by TJ International Ltd, Padstow, Cornwall

Contents

Foreword   v

Introduction   1
Steering group members   5
How is NICE guidance issued?   9
Steps towards implementation   13
Who is responsible for managing the implementation
    of NICE guidance?   15
Initiating implementation   17
Assessing resource implications of guidance   21
Developing an action plan   25
Who should be involved in the implementation process?   27
Developing a local approach to implementing guidance   29
Circulating guidance and publicising action plans   33
Using successful strategies for implementing guidance   35
Monitoring guidance implementation   39
Evaluation and audit of guidance implementation   43
Feedback   45

Appendix 1 Checklists and aids   47
Appendix 2 Practical examples   91
Appendix 3 What is NICE? What is the NPC? What is CHI?   113
Appendix 4 Focus group members and other
    acknowledgements   121
Appendix 5 How this handbook was produced   131

Bibliography   135
Abbreviations   137
Index   139

Foreword

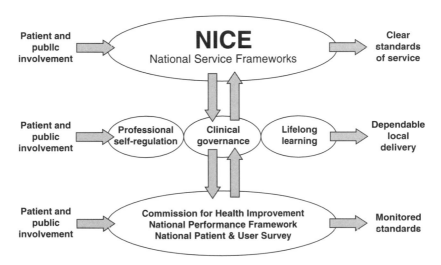

Setting, delivering & monitoring standards

The Government and Welsh Assembly have reshaped the NHS with an overall agenda for improving the quality of healthcare. The model sets clear national standards, with local responsibility for delivery, backed by consistent monitoring arrangements.

NICE – The National Institute for Clinical Excellence – was established as a Special Health Authority for England and Wales in April 1999. As part of the National Health Service (NHS) its role is to provide patients, health professionals and the public with authoritative, robust and reliable guidance on current 'best practice'.

Good clinical guidance, if properly developed, disseminated and implemented, improves the healthcare of the population as a whole and supports health professionals in doing their best for individual patients.

NICE guidance will cover both individual health technologies and the clinical management of specific conditions. We will ensure that the technology appraisals and guidelines we develop are based on robust research findings, address cost as well as clinical effectiveness and are distributed to clinicians and patients in a form that will be useful on a day to day basis.

NICE guidance will be published at a significant rate over the next few years; up to 20 clinical guidelines and 50 technology appraisals per year, and each piece is important. As a consequence, careful planning for effective implementation is now a crucial task for all NHS organisations.

Whilst NICE does not have a remit for implementation of its guidance, it wants to help those that do. Therefore, the Institute has supported the National Prescribing Centre in the production of this handbook, to assist you with the local implementation of our guidance.

This handbook is a practical guide for NHS clinicians and managers on how to adopt and monitor national guidance. Developed with NHS staff working at the coal-face, it looks at the roles and responsibilities of key individuals in health service organisations, and provides useful examples, checklists and frameworks for ensuring NICE guidance is translated into local action.

Whether you are actively involved in managing the implementation of guidance, or you just need to know what is going on, this handbook is essential reading and I commend it to you.

Professor Sir Michael Rawlins
Chair, National Institute for Clinical Excellence
July 2001

Introduction

What is this handbook?

First, lets be clear about what this handbook is not. It is *not* a piece of formal NICE guidance, nor is it intended to be a bible of implementation. This handbook is intended to be a practical guide for NHS clinicians and managers on how to adopt and monitor guidance produced by the National Institute for Clinical Excellence (NICE). However, it may also be of value in helping to implement other key guidance, such as National Service Frameworks (NSFs) issued by the Department of Health.

It looks at the potential roles and responsibilities of key individuals within organisations, and identifies frameworks for ensuring that guidance is translated into local action.

Throughout the handbook there are examples of how people are handling guidance implementation across the NHS. These examples are not necessarily proven good practice, but are included to help readers develop their own ideas. Each example includes a contact person who is willing to expand on their experiences. It may be that they will tell you what worked well but importantly they may also explain the pitfalls and what didn't go as well as expected!

The handbook also contains checklists and aids that can be tailored to specific circumstances. These checklists and aids will also be placed on the National Prescribing Centre (NPC) web site (www.npc.co.uk) so that they can be downloaded, adapted and printed off as required.

How to use this handbook

This handbook is not designed to be read all at once, and certainly not from cover to cover. We are sure that not all of it will be of interest to everyone. It is designed to flick through, to allow you to pick up tips, identify support on key issues, work through your own ideas using other's frameworks, and also as a reference and guide.

Each section includes a Key Points box, plus suggestions as to who may take on the roles described. Throughout the book the following symbols are used to guide you towards:

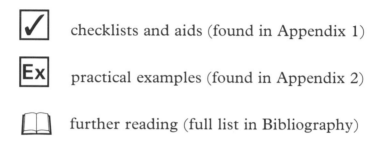

✓   checklists and aids (found in Appendix 1)

Ex   practical examples (found in Appendix 2)

📖   further reading (full list in Bibliography)

Who is this handbook for?

If you are involved in healthcare at a clinical or managerial level, this handbook is for you – to support you as you manage the implementation of NICE guidance. It is aimed at those actively involved in the process and those who just need to know what is going on. It will help to answer questions such as *What should I be doing?* and *Who should I ask?*

Where do the ideas in this handbook come from?

The content is based on the ideas and experience of those working in the NHS today, gathered through a wide-ranging consultation process. In addition, it has drawn on the expertise of NICE and the NPC.

It has been actively developed by a steering group whose members are facing the same issues as you (*see* pp. 5–8).

In addition to the central guidance you receive from the Department of Health or the National Assembly for Wales, NICE will be producing around 50 pieces of technology appraisal guidance and 20 clinical guidelines each year. This handbook should help everyone involved with the implementation of them.

Further reading

Implementing clinical practice guidelines: can guidelines be used to improve clinical practice? *Effective Health Care* **1**(8). NHS Centre for Reviews and Dissemination, 1994.

Steering group members

Kim Brackley MSc MRPharmS
Kim is Principal Pharmacist for London Pharmacy Education and Training. She is involved in the design and provision of training to assist in the delivery and development of services in primary and secondary care.

Paul Clark FRPharmS
Paul was an independent community pharmacist contractor, Secretary of St Helens & Knowsley LPC and pharmaceutical member of St Helens & Knowsley FPC, FHSA and Health Authority. He is currently Prescribing Support Pharmacist for West Lancashire PCG, and Primary Care Pharmacist for St Helens South PCG. He is a non-executive director of St Helens & Knowsley Hospitals Trust.

Linda Goulden SRN DN
Linda is a Practice Nurse in South Manchester. She became a PCG Board Nurse and was then appointed Member of the Professional Executive Committee when South Manchester PCG became a first wave Trust in April 2000. She is Joint Clinical Governance Lead and one of the professional representatives on the Trust Board.

Dr Stephen Henderson MbChB
Stephen is a practising GP in South Manchester. He was Deputy Chair of South Manchester PCG that became a PCT in April 2000.

Clive Jackson MSc MRPharmS **(Chairman)**
Clive is Director of the National Prescribing Centre and was previously Regional Prescribing Adviser for North West Regional Health Authority. He also spent time on secondment to the NHS Executive, working on prescribing issues and policies.

Nicola John MPhil DMS MRPharmS
Nicola is Director of Pharmaceutical Public Health for Iechyd Morgannwg Health Authority. She provides advice on all aspects of medicines management for both primary and secondary care.

Professor Elizabeth Kay MSc MRPharmS
Liz is Head of Pharmacy Services, Leeds Teaching Hospitals NHS Trust and Professor of Hospital Pharmacy, University of Bradford. She is involved with local implementation of NICE guidance.

Dr Paul Miller BM BCh MSc DPhil FRCP
Paul is Consultant Gastroenterologist and Director of the Lipid Clinic at The South Manchester University Hospitals NHS Trust, where he is also Chairman of the Clinical Governance Committee.

Dr Paul Myres M Med SC
Paul is a GP in North Wales and Primary Care Adviser to the Clinical Effectiveness Support Unit in Wales. He was an active member of North Wales MAAG and is a former GP CME tutor.

Mark Pilling MPhil MRPharmS
Mark is Head of Clinical Governance and Prescribing for Kirkby PCG in Knowsley, Merseyside. He was previously a Primary Care Pharmacist, supporting a GP Commissioning Group, and prior to that Pharmaceutical Adviser to St Helens & Knowsley Health Authority.

Marilyn Ramsden MRPharmS
Marilyn is Chief Pharmaceutical Adviser to North and East Devon Health Authority. She was previously Pharmaceutical Adviser for Somerset FHSA. Her pharmaceutical experience includes work in both hospital and community settings.

Anne-Toni Rodgers BSc(Hons) MIIIM
Anne-Toni is Communications Director for the National Institute for Clinical Excellence. Before joining NICE she worked in a variety of areas, including pure research, regulatory affairs, sales & marketing, and government & industry affairs. Prior to joining the Institute she was Head of National Healthcare Development for AstraZeneca Pharmaceuticals.

Donna Sager BA(Hons) MSc
Donna is Chief Executive of West Stockport PCG and was previously Primary Care Manager at the NHS Executive North West. She has a specific interest in prescribing and incorporating this work into general management.

Richard Seal BSc(Hons) MCPP Dip Pres Sci MRPharmS
Richard is Pharmaceutical Adviser to Birmingham Health Authority. Formerly, he was a Hospital Clinical Pharmacist specialising in drug information and intensive care medicine. Richard has recently been appointed as an NPC Training Adviser in therapeutics.

Rachel Webb MSc MRPharmS
Rachel is Prescribing Adviser to Huntingdonshire PCG. She has been a Pharmaceutical Adviser since 1991 and has worked for a number of FHSAs and HAs.

Stephen Wright MB ChB FRCGP AFOM DObstRCOG
Stephen is the Medical Adviser to Rotherham Health Authority and was previously in full-time general practice. He is also a General Medical Council performance assessor and is on the Board of the Medical Managers in Primary Care group of the British Association of Medical Managers.

Project design and management

Helen Critchlow BSc(Hons) MRPharmS MCPP Dip Pres Sci

Helen is a consultant pharmacist working with the NHS and also in the development of computerised clinical decision support systems. She was previously Pharmaceutical Adviser to Bury & Rochdale Health Authority.

Administrative support

Annette Ireland

Annette has worked for the National Prescribing Centre since it was created in April 1996. She is currently Personal Assistant to the Director at the National Prescribing Centre.

How is NICE guidance issued?

Guidance is issued by NICE in a number of forms, for example:

- clinical guidelines
- technology appraisals
- referral advice.

Each is made available in different presentations for different audiences.

NICE has a statutory duty under the Welsh Language Act and ensures that the summary guidance and patient texts are available in Welsh.

NICE guidance can be obtained from their web site (www.nice.org.uk) or by telephoning the NHS Response Line 08701 555 455.

How NICE guidance will be disseminated

- The NICE web site will publish all guidance as it is released. The web site will include newsflashes to indicate when a new piece of guidance has been issued. It also provides the facility for individuals to register for automatic emails, in order that they are alerted when new guidance is published.
- A copy of the NICE web site will also be available on the NHSnet.
- There is a core mailing list for each piece of guidance. This includes chief executives of NHS trusts, health authorities and primary care organisations.
- In addition, each piece of guidance has its own targeted mailing list (the full mailing list is printed inside its front cover).

Other dissemination routes include:

- the media
- PRODIGY
- NHS Direct on-line
- National Electronic Library for Health
- patient newsletters
- patient/carer organisations
- partnerships with other 'closed' web sites
- every six months a 'compilation' of all NICE's products will be published and circulated to healthcare professionals.

Whilst NICE does not have a remit for implementation of its guidance, it wants to be sure that take-up is both widespread and efficient. Therefore NICE has supported the NPC in the production of this handbook, to assist in the local implementation of its guidance.

Further reading

What is NICE? (Appendix 3)
What is the NPC? (Appendix 3)

Note: NICE guidance covers England and Wales. In Wales, local health groups have been established; in England, primary care groups and primary care trusts. Recognising that there are various terms to describe these organisations, the term 'primary care organisation' (PCO) will be used throughout this handbook. Similarly, local committees and groups are referred to frequently. These groups will have different titles in different areas but throughout the handbook we have attempted to use commonly understood titles. The term 'patient/carer representation' is used to cover any patient or carer groups or the public who are concerned with the provision of healthcare in England and Wales. Throughout the handbook 'key stakeholders' are also referred to, and these include patient/carer organisations where appropriate. Similarly, we have used the term 'professional advisers' to include amongst others medical and pharmaceutical prescribing advisers.

Steps towards implementation

This handbook has been written as a series of 'steps' to consider when NICE guidance is issued. Some of these steps will be more or less relevant, depending on the nature of the guidance. They have been presented in a logical order but the process should be flexible and responsive to local needs. The steps are summarised overleaf, and each step is then described in more detail in the following pages.

Who is responsible for managing the
implementation of NICE guidance?

↓

Initiating implementation

↓

Assessing resource implications
of guidance

↓

Developing an action plan

↓

Who should be involved
in the implementation process?

↓

Developing a local approach to
implementing guidance

↓

Circulating guidance and
publicising action plans

↓

Using successful strategies for
implementing guidance

↓

Monitoring guidance implementation

↓

Evaluation and audit of
guidance implementation

↓

Feedback

Education and continuing professional development will be crucial
elements of successful implementation of national guidance. Their
potential to support this process should be considered at each stage.

Who is responsible for managing the implementation of NICE guidance?

> **Key points**
>
> - One single focus, defined in advance, should be given the responsibility for initiating and co-ordinating local action on all NICE guidance. A named lead may be nominated for a specific piece of guidance.
> - A working group, existing or new, may need to be identified.
> - Organisations should work together to avoid duplication of effort.

While the Chief Executive of each NHS organisation is accountable for the implementation of all NICE guidance, practical responsibility for this should rest with one appropriate individual or group, acting as the 'focus' locally. This will avoid the situation where NICE guidance is 'someone else's responsibility' or where everybody starts 'doing his or her own thing'.

The role of this focus should be to co-ordinate any workload arising across organisations, relevant groups and individuals. The expertise and resources available within existing groups should be used wherever possible. On occasions, the focus may nominate a lead person to manage the activity on a specific piece of guidance. This lead should have local credibility and the visible backing of the relevant chief executives. It is always important that workload, which could be significant, is delegated effectively.

Asking the following questions may be beneficial:

- Do you know who is responsible for initiating and co-ordinating NICE guidance implementation across your local-ity/organisation?
- Do you know who is taking the lead for each specific piece of guidance?
- Do others in your organisation know?

Organisations (health authorities, PCOs and trusts) should work together to avoid duplication of effort. It is therefore important to define the locality across which the work is to be co-ordinated. This will depend on local geographical and organisational boundaries.

Examples of who could be the single focus for NICE guidance

- Clinical Governance Leads.
- Director of Public Health.
- Medical/Nursing Director.
- Director of Quality.

 Practical examples

A diagrammatic representation of guidance implementation (Appendix 1)

How different organisations are delegating responsibility for NICE guidance (Appendix 2)

📖 **Further reading**

A First Class Service: quality in the new NHS. Department of Health, 1998.

Putting Patients First. NHS Wales, January 1998.

Initiating implementation

Key points

- Check published work plans where available. The NICE forward work plan is published on their web site.
- Consider the implementation of guidance with an agreed timetable.
- Consider prioritisation of local initiatives to coincide with the issue of NICE guidance.
- Publicise any implementation plan.
- Ensure that there is co-operation across different organisations, geographical areas and different healthcare environments.

National guidance has been, and always will be, a part of the NHS. NICE guidance will be published at a significant rate over the next few years; up to 20 clinical guidelines and 50 technology appraisals per year. NICE guidance has to be considered alongside other programmes, such as NSFs, Strategic and Financial Frameworks (SaFFs) and Health Improvement Programmes (HImPs/HIP), in terms of financial, service and other implications. Planning for implementation of NICE guidance should be incorporated into the commissioning and financial planning frameworks of each organisation.

Every piece of guidance is important. Planned approaches to implementation should be publicised to all key stakeholders, including the public.

Remember, each organisation should take account of its neighbouring organisations. There will be many pieces of guidance that would be best implemented in a co-ordinated way across localities. Implementation processes should use local clinical and managerial networks, working across different levels and organisations.

Examples of those who may be involved in planning for NICE guidance locally

- Clinical Governance Leads/Committees.
- Public Health.
- Professional Advisers.
- Professional Executive Committee of PCOs.
- Medical/Nursing Director, Lead Clinical/Consultant, Chief Pharmacist.
- Area Prescribing Committee.
- Drug & Therapeutics Committee.

Processes which need to be linked into planning for implementation

- Needs assessment.
- HImP/HIP development.
- Commissioning and Financial Planning, e.g. SaFF.
- Implementation of NSFs.

  Checklists and aids

The NICE work programme (Appendix 1)

Individuals and groups who may be involved in the implementation of NICE guidance (Appendix 1)

Questions which may help planning for implementation of each piece of guidance (Appendix 1)

Practical examples

Initiating implementation (Appendix 2)

Further reading

Health Improvement Programmes: core guidance and framework documents. Issued with WHC (2000) 001. Health Service Strategy 1, National Assembly for Wales. 28 January 2000.

Health Improvement Programmes and Long-Term Agreements: guidance. WHC (1999) 087. 29 June 1999.

Joint Priorities for Health and Social Services. Guidance from the National Assembly for Wales (in preparation).

Modernising Health and Social Services: National Priorities Guidance 2000/01–2002/03. HSC 1999/242, LAC(99)38. 21 December 1999. This identifies effective use of NICE guidance as part of the quality agenda for modernising the NHS.

Planning for Health and Health Care: incorporating guidance for Health and Local Authorities on Health Improvement Programmes, Service and Financial Frameworks, Joint Investment Plans and Primary Care Investment Plans. HSC 1999/244, LAC(99)39. 21 December 1999.

Assessing resource implications of guidance

> **Key points**
>
> - Identify what is current local practice for a piece of guidance, using local information and expertise.
> - Identify the resource implications of implementing this guidance.

The implementation of NICE guidance will usually have some financial, service and/or workforce implications. There may be a requirement for additional funding, or the potential to release existing resources for reinvestment elsewhere. However, practical experience is that the process of disinvestment can be lengthy.

A useful example is the NICE guidance on proton pump inhibitors which has implications for the way *Helicobacter* status is investigated. There may be contracting/commissioning implications for endoscopy services, including referrals, capacity and waiting times, and for histopathology services.

It should also be remembered that the implementation process itself may require resourcing. In addition, when considering the local financial and service implications of NICE guidance, any national directives or targeted support should be taken into account.

Funding implications should be identified as early as possible. Health authorities, PCOs and trusts all have financial systems in place for managing in-year pressures. Any financial implications that might arise from the implementation of NICE guidance should be fed into the planning process.

Examples of who may be involved in considering the resource implications

- Clinical Governance Leads/Committees.
- Finance Directors.
- Finance and Commissioning Groups.
- Director of Public Health.
- Clinical Audit Leads.
- Professional Advisers.
- Professional Executive Committees of PCOs.
- Medical/Nursing Director, Clinical Director/Lead Clinician/Consultant, Chief Pharmacist.
- HImP/HIP Groups.
- Area Prescribing Committee.
- Drug & Therapeutics Committee.

 Checklists and aids

Individuals and groups who may be involved in the implementation of NICE guidance (Appendix 1)
Examples of local resources/staff which may be affected by implementation of NICE guidance (Appendix 1)

 Practical examples

Assessing the resource implications of guidance (Appendix 2)

 Further reading

Planning for Health and Health Care: incorporating guidance for Health and Local Authorities on Health Improvement

Programmes, Service and Financial Frameworks, Joint Investment Plans and Primary Care Investment Plans. HSC 1999/244, LAC(99)39. 21 December 1999.

Department of Health Letter to Chief Executives of Health Authorities – allocation of extra resources for 2000/01. 28.3.00.

Developing an action plan

Key points

- Identify all key stakeholders.
- Involve all key stakeholders in the planning and implementation process.
- Draw up and agree a plan which lists key action points and then agree milestones and timescales.

Those with delegated responsibility for managing the activity on a specific piece of guidance should develop an agreed action plan for the implementation process. Everyone should share a common understanding of what the action plan is setting out to achieve, and have the opportunity to participate in its development. This approach shares out the workload and can increase the commitment of all participants. Any implementation plan needs to be linked into the routine planning and management frameworks of the organisations involved.

The plan may be simple, for example where the guidance recommends that a technology is not used, or it may be more complex for some clinical guidelines. Each stage of the plan should include milestones with dates for completion. This is essential for monitoring progress.

Consideration needs to be given to having the action plan formally approved by the relevant Boards or Committees.

Examples of who might help develop an action plan

- Area Prescribing Committee.
- Clinical Governance Committee.
- Medical/Nursing Director.
- Clinical Specialists.
- Director of Public Health.
- Professional Advisers.
- Professional Executive Committee of PCOs.
- PCO Prescribing Groups.
- Drug & Therapeutics Committee.
- Educational Leads.
- Relevant Patient/Carer Representation.

 Checklists and aids

Individuals and groups who may be involved in the implementation of NICE guidance (Appendix 1)

Developing an action plan – examples of what to consider (Appendix 1)

An example checklist to support the process of guidance implementation in clinical teams (Appendix 1)

 Practical examples

How different organisations have developed their action plans (Appendix 2)

Who should be involved in the implementation process?

Key points

- Identify key stakeholders to be involved in the implementation of each piece of guidance.
- Ensure co-operative working across all levels and organisations.

Everyone should be involved! Obvious but easy to forget is the fact that implementation of NICE guidance is often likely to impact at all levels throughout the NHS.

Those with delegated responsibility for managing the activity on a specific piece of guidance should identify key stakeholders to be involved in implementation within each organisation. The selection of these key stakeholders will depend on the nature and content of the guidance. However, it may be that a core group could be tasked with actioning all of one specific type of guidance. New groups or structures should **not** be set up when existing ones could fulfil the required roles.

On occasions, it may be appropriate for one organisation to be nominated to take the lead; for example, when a particular piece of guidance relates to a regionally-based specialist service. Such nominations are likely to be in line with lead commissioning arrangements.

Examples of who may be key to implementing NICE guidance

- Clinical Governance Leads/Committees.
- Director of Public Health.
- Professional Advisers.
- Medical/Nursing Director.
- Lead Health Professionals.
- PCO GP Leads.
- Local Professional Committees.
- Area Prescribing Committee.
- Drug & Therapeutics Committee.
- Clinical Effectiveness Team.
- Educational Leads.
- Regional Teams/Leads.

 Checklists and aids

Individuals and groups who may be involved in the implementation of NICE guidance (Appendix 1)

Steps towards implementation – who could be involved at each stage? (Appendix 1)

 Practical examples

Who is being involved in the implementation of NICE guidance? (Appendix 2)

Developing a local approach to implementing guidance

> **Key point**
>
> - Consider how implementation of NICE guidance should be achieved locally.

Implementation of NICE guidance may need to be fine-tuned in light of local circumstances. It may be that achieving full implementation involves a long-term commitment to significant change, e.g. a small capital development, plus a shorter-term plan, which may involve partial implementation of the guidance. To deliver this, those elements of the guidance that are already in place locally, and those that are not, should be identified. Any such process needs to be robust, with transparent systems for agreeing local implementation.

Decisions to modify NICE guidance must be transparent and defensible if challenged. In these circumstances, it should be documented that the guidance has been considered and that there is a justifiable reason why alternative action has been taken. A reasonable test is whether any modification could, if challenged, be justified in Court, given the expert and authoritative nature of the guidance.

Where current practice varies from NICE guidance, this variance should be addressed rather than the guidance being altered to suit local circumstances. Certain guidance may mean that local choices have to be made. For example, the NICE guidance on the use of hip prostheses for total hip replacement does not identify a single product; rather, it sets a benchmark for revisions and establishes the data requirements to meet the benchmark. The NHS Purchasing and Supplies Authority have created a database of all the hip joint replacements that meet this guidance and it is available on the NHSnet to inform local decision making.

It is important to note that national guidance may explain its particular status. For example, each piece of NICE technology appraisal guidance includes a statement about its status – the guidance on wisdom teeth removal stated:

'This guidance represents the view of the Institute's Appraisal Committee, which was arrived at after careful consideration of the available evidence. Health professionals are expected to take it fully into account when exercising their clinical judgement about the circumstances in which it is appropriate to consider the removal of wisdom teeth. This guidance does not, however, override the individual responsibility of health professionals to make appropriate decisions in the circumstances of the individual patient, in consultation with the patient and/ or guardian or carer.'

Examples of who may be involved in developing a local approach to implementation

- Clinical Governance Leads/Committees.
- Director of Public Health and Professional Advisers.
- Professional Executive Committee of PCOs and GP Prescribing Leads.
- Medical/Nursing Director, Clinical Director, Guidelines Co-ordinator, Chief Pharmacist.
- HImP/HIP Groups.
- Area Prescribing Committee.
- Drug & Therapeutics Committee.
- Educational Leads.

✓ **Checklists and aids**

Individuals and groups who may be involved in the implementation of NICE guidance (Appendix 1)

An example of a 'recommendation proforma' for implementing guidance (Appendix 1)

Circulating guidance and publicising action plans

Key points

- Identify who has received guidance directly from NICE.
- Circulate the guidance to others locally as necessary.
- Inform healthcare professionals and managers about local implementation plans.

NICE will circulate their guidance widely, as described earlier. For each piece of guidance, a circulation list is printed inside the front cover.

However, there is still a need to identify who has and who ought to have received the guidance locally. Those with delegated responsibility for managing the activity on a specific piece of guidance should identify a system to circulate it to selected individuals and groups. These individuals and groups should then be responsible for onward circulation to their colleagues, and be encouraged to confirm that the information has been received. This cascade system should be widely publicised so that everyone knows where information is coming from and to whom feedback should be given.

The next step is to publicise the local action plan. Whilst alone this activity is unlikely to lead to appropriate changes in behaviour, awareness and understanding play a crucial part in the overall implementation process (*see* pp. 35–8).

Some guidance may have gained a high profile in the national media. In these cases, communication teams within your organisation may have a particularly important role in publicising agreed local activity and response.

Examples of those who might be involved in circulating NICE guidance and publicising action plans locally

- Clinical Governance and/or Prescribing Lead.
- Professional Advisers and/or Director of Public Health.
- Trust Clinical Director and/or Chief Pharmacist.
- Local Professional Committees.
- Communications Leads.
- Educational Leads.
- Information Leads.

 Checklists and aids

Who has received guidance directly from NICE and who else needs to see it? (Appendix 1)

Tips for local circulation of NICE guidance (Appendix 1)

 Practical examples

How NICE guidance is being circulated locally (Appendix 2)

 Further reading

Effective Health Care: getting evidence into practice. NHS Centre for Reviews and Dissemination. February 1999, Volume 5, Number 1.

Using successful strategies for implementing guidance

Key points

- Consult widely.
- Get key stakeholders on board.
- Ensure that implementation programmes use proven intervention techniques.
- Sustain change over time.

Successful implementation of guidance, even if it has been developed nationally, requires healthcare professionals and managers to have 'ownership' of the process and outcomes locally.

The Department of Health, the National Assembly for Wales, Royal Colleges and other professional bodies may provide additional advice to their health professionals on issues around specific NICE guidance. However, all professions should ensure that there are effective local mechanisms to gather their corporate views on the implications that such guidance may have on their practice (examples include budgetary impact and training requirements). These views should then be communicated to those ultimately responsible for implementing the NICE guidance.

Barriers to change can be formidable, but implementation programmes can be successful if they use proven interventions.

An *Effective Health Care Bulletin* was devoted to a review of the literature concerned with changing professional practice. It concluded that a range of interventions have been shown to be effective in changing professional behaviour in some circumstances. Multiple interventions, targeting different barriers to change, are more likely to be effective than single ones.

Successful strategies for changing practice should be adequately resourced, and will require people with appropriate knowledge and skills. Any systematic approach to changing professional practice should include plans to monitor, evaluate, maintain, review and reinforce any change. For any large-scale programme of change to be effective, a range of interventions, usually spanning 3–5 years, is needed.

Examples of who may be key to managing change

- Clinical Governance Leads/Committees.
- Professional Advisers.
- Professional Executive Committees of PCOs.
- GP Prescribing Leads and Groups, GPs.
- Medical/Nursing Director, Clinical Director, Chief Pharmacist, Consultants.
- Community Pharmacists, Practice Nurses.
- Area Prescribing Committee.
- Educational Leads.
- NSF and HImP/HIP Groups.
- Local Professional Committees.

 Checklists and aids

Some practical tips for implementing guidance and managing required change (Appendix 1)

Useful web sites (Appendix 1)

📖 Further reading

There is a wealth of published literature on the subject of managing change and the successful implementation of guidance in healthcare. The following list is by no means exhaustive but guides the reader to some of the most well-recognised resources.

Area Prescribing Committees: maintaining effectiveness in the modern NHS. A guide to good practice. First Edition. National Prescribing Centre, September 2000.

Clinical Guidelines: using clinical guidelines to improve patient care within the NHS. NHS Executive, 1996.

Effective Health Care: getting evidence into practice. NHS Centre for Reviews and Dissemination. February 1999, Volume 5, Number 1.

Experience, Evidence and Everyday Practice: creating systems for delivering effective health care. Dunning, M *et al.* King's Fund, 1999. The King's Fund PACE programme (Promoting Action on Clinical Effectiveness) is formed of 16 development projects around England working to turn evidence into everyday clinical practice. This book is based on their work, and gives 10 essential practical tasks for managing change, including advice about using different techniques to achieve change in clinical practice.

Learning from FACTS: Lessons from the Framework for Appropriate Care Throughout Sheffield (FACTS) Project. Eve, R *et al.* School of Health and Related Research, University of Sheffield, 1997.

The Front-Line Evidence-Based Medicine Project: Final Report. Donald, A. NHS Executive North Thames Regional Office R&D, 1998. Explores the feasibility of using evidence in daily clinical practice and the infrastructure required to support this. Concludes that in almost all cases the most formidable barriers to the use of evidence in clinical practice were structural and logistical problems (e.g. IT availability and training) rather than behavioural problems of clinicians.

Getting Better with Evidence: experiences of putting evidence into practice. King's Fund and NHS Executive, 2000. http://www.doh.gov.uk/ntrd/getbtr.htm#2

Getting Research Findings into Practice. Haines, A. BMJ Books, 1998.

GP Prescribing Support: a resource document and guide for the New NHS. NPC and NHS Executive, 1998. A review of the effectiveness of various interventions for altering prescribing behaviour.

Implementing Evidence-based Changes in Healthcare. Evans, D and Haines, A (eds). Radcliffe Medical Press, 2000.

Managing Antibiotic Resistance: a practical guide. NPC and Edgecumbe Health, 2000. This pack contains a lot of useful information about leading change, motivating and influencing PCOs and primary healthcare teams.

Monitoring guidance implementation

Key points

- Monitor the progress of guidance implementation against agreed milestones.
- Identify any problems or barriers to successful implementation.
- Use the results of monitoring to refine the current action plan and to inform future implementation processes.

All stages in the action plan should be monitored against agreed milestones and outcomes. It is important to ensure that uptake of guidance is happening, and if not, to find out why not. Progress should be publicised, e.g. by word of mouth at meetings, by local newsletter or intranets/web sites.

Outcome measures can take many forms. It is not always possible to see the real clinical outcome from an intervention in the short to medium term. In these cases, proxy outcome indicators may need to be used. For example, a reduction in cholesterol levels is often used as a proxy for the effect that 'statins' have on mortality rates from coronary heart disease.

The indicators themselves will depend on the nature of the guidance – some guidance will recommend specific outcome measures. If guidance involves the discontinuation of a particular technology, monitoring could simply involve identifying where that technology is still being used. It is also important to monitor whether any problems, or barriers to change, are being addressed.

Clinical governance frameworks should already include monitoring processes for effects on:

- patient outcomes
- service delivery and development
- reconfiguration of existing services
- financial resources (including the cost of monitoring)
- workforce
- training and education
- other resources.

Using readily available sources of information can facilitate monitoring and, on occasions, reduce the need for formal audit. Examples of standard information sources include prescribing data, PRIMIS/MIQUEST, disease registers and clinical information systems. Significant event analysis and complaints data are other useful monitoring tools.

Regional bodies and the Commission for Health Improvement (CHI) will also be monitoring NHS organisations for progress on implementation of NICE guidance. The Secretary of State for Health has indicated that in England the Department of Health will be monitoring the implementation of NICE guidance at 1 month and 6 months post launch.

Examples of who might monitor the implementation of NICE guidance

- Clinical Audit Leads.
- Audit Advisory Groups.
- Clinical Governance Facilitators.
- Public Health Department.
- Information Departments.
- Professional Advisers.
- Trust Clinical Teams, Chief Pharmacist.
- All professionals and managers.

Checklists and aids

Individuals and groups who may be involved in the implementation of NICE guidance (Appendix 1)

An example template for monitoring the implementation process (Appendix 1)

Examples of data sources available for use in monitoring, audit and evaluation (Appendix 1)

 Practical examples

Monitoring guidance implementation (Appendix 2)

 Further reading

What is CHI? (Appendix 3)

Primary Care Groups and Prescribing Data: using MIQUEST software. National Prescribing Centre Information Resource, September 1999.

Practical Clinical Governance in Primary Care: managing antibiotic prescribing: audit handbook. National Prescribing Centre, March 2000.

Clinical Guidelines: using clinical guidelines to improve patient care within the NHS. NHS Executive, 1996.

Evaluation and audit of guidance implementation

Key points

- Audit methodologies may be included within the NICE guidance.
- Select which guidance, or elements of guidance, are most relevant and important to local healthcare.
- Develop methods of structured audit appropriate for your area.

Clinical audit is one method for ensuring that organisations are doing what they think they are doing. It is part of a development process and can provide valuable information to determine if guidance has been actioned locally, and is being followed in practice.

Where audit methodologies from NICE are included, they will not normally be prescriptive. Similar audits may already have been undertaken locally which broadly meet these requirements. On occasion, a nationally co-ordinated audit will be recommended.

Clinical governance planning within an organisation should encompass the commissioning or execution of audits, including audit of NICE guidance. Audit resources are generally limited and such audits, where appropriate, must be planned for well in advance.

Some NICE guidance may not have been implemented immediately, or, alternatively, staff may consider that they are already complying with the guidance. Be aware that data to support any local position will probably be required on review.

Examples of who might be involved in the audit and evaluation of NICE guidance implementation

- Clinical Audit Leads.
- Audit Advisory Groups.
- Clinical Governance Facilitators.
- Public Health Department.
- Information Departments.
- Professional Advisers.
- Trust Clinical Teams, Chief Pharmacist.
- All professionals and managers involved in clinical care (e.g. GPs, Community Pharmacists, Practice Nurses).

 Checklists and aids

Examples of data sources available for use in monitoring, audit and evaluation (Appendix 1)

 Further reading

Practical Clinical Governance in Primary Care: managing antibiotic prescribing: audit handbook. National Prescribing Centre, March 2000.

Feedback

Key points

- Feedback on achievements is important; progress on implementation, and its results, should be publicised.
- All those affected by the changes, including the public, should be encouraged to provide feedback on their experiences.
- Relevant feedback should be provided to the originating organisation to inform the development of future guidance (e.g. to NICE).

There is no point collecting and analysing data if the results are not publicised. Positive feedback is as important as negative feedback. If good practice is already in place, this information should be shared.

Mechanisms for feedback include:

- regular monitoring reports presented at Board level
- team meetings
- public meetings
- local professional committees
- newsletters
- educational meetings
- clinical networks
- local web site/email
- clinical governance networks web site
- NICE web site/email.

The feedback on each implementation plan should also be combined to highlight progress on the overall programme of change.

Feedback should work both ways, so that local performance can be compared with other localities, and also with the national position. Feedback may also help to inform research and development (R&D) programmes, where formal research could be identified as necessary to fill gaps in existing knowledge.

Examples of who might feed back the results of guidance implementation

- Clinical Governance Leads/Committees/Facilitators.
- Clinical Audit Leads.
- Professional Advisers.
- Public Health.
- PCO Prescribing Leads and Groups.
- Trust Medical Director, Clinical Directors, Chief Pharmacist.
- NSF and HImP/HIP Groups.
- Local Professional Committees.
- Educational Leads.
- Communications Leads.
- All professionals and managers involved in clinical care.
- Patient/carer representation.

  Checklists and aids

An example template for feeding back the results of guidance implementation at Board level (Appendix 1)

Appendix 1
Checklists and aids

A diagrammatic representation of guidance
   implementation   49
The NICE work programme (May 2001)   50
Individuals and groups who may be involved in
   the implementation of NICE guidance   52
Questions which may help with planning for
   implementation of each piece of guidance   56
Examples of local resources/staff which may be affected by
   implementation of NICE guidance   58
Developing an action plan – examples of what
   to consider   59
An example checklist to support the process of
   guidance implementation in clinical teams   68
Steps towards implementation – who could be
   involved at each stage?   69
An example of a 'recommendation proforma' for
   implementing guidance   71
Who has received guidance directly from NICE and
   who else needs to see it?   72
Tips for local circulation of NICE guidance   79
Some practical tips for implementing guidance and
   managing required change   81

An example template for monitoring the
    implementation process   85
Examples of data sources available for use in monitoring,
    audit and evaluation   86
An example template for feeding back the results of
    guidance implementation at Board level   87
Useful web sites   88

Please note that the checklists marked with ✓ **are available on the NPC web site for downloading and customisation purposes (www.npc.co.uk).**

A diagrammatic representation of guidance implementation

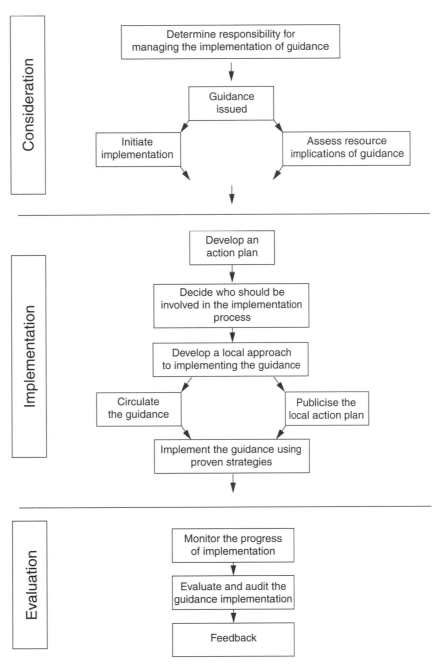

The NICE work programme (May 2001)

Technology Appraisals	Date expected?
• Rituximab for follicular lymphoma and chronic lymphocytic lymphoma	June 2001
• Irinotecan, Oxaliplatin, Raltitrexed drugs for colorectal cancer	June 2001
• Docetaxel, Paclitaxel, Gemcitabine and Vinorelbine for lung cancer	June 2001
• Cox II inhibitors for arthritis	June 2001
• Trastuzumab and Vinorelbine for breast cancer	July 2001
• Topotecan for ovarian cancer	July 2001
• Fludarabine for follicular lymphoma and chronic lymphocytic lymphoma	September 2001
• Beta interferon and Glatiramer for multiple sclerosis	September 2001
• Review of Taxanes for breast and ovarian cancer	September 2001 (Ovarian on hold, existing guidance continues to apply)
• Etanercept and Infliximab for rheumatoid arthritis	October 2001
• Infliximab for Crohn's disease	November 2001
• Newer atypical antipsychotics for schizophrenia	December 2001
• Inhaler devices for asthma in older children	December 2001
• Bupropion (zyban) and NRT for smoking cessation	March 2002
• Routine Anti-D prophylaxis in pregnancy	April 2002
• Human Growth Hormone for children and adults	April 2002

Technology Appraisals	Date expected?
• Metal-on-metal hip resurfacing	May 2002
• Caelyx for ovarian cancer	May 2002
• Ramipril (Tritace) for CHD	May 2002
• CBT for depression and anxiety	June 2002
• Surgery for morbid obesity	June 2002
• Ultrasonic venous line locating devices	July 2002
• Verteporfin and SnET2 for age related macular degeneration	July 2002
• STI-571 for leukaemia	August 2002
• Tenecteplase for out of hospital treatment of myocardial infarction	September 2002

Clinical Guidelines

See NICE web site for details.

All dates are provisional as the process NICE follows allows for consultation and appeal if required.

This list was correct as at May 2001. Check the NICE web site (www.nice.org.uk) for the latest version.

☑ **Individuals and groups who may be involved in the implementation of NICE guidance**

These lists were compiled in brainstorming sessions during the development of this handbook. Please note that these lists are not exhaustive and in different organisations titles may vary. You may wish to customise these lists for your own local use.

Title of Guidance document: _____

HEALTH AUTHORITY	Yes (✓)	No (✓)
Chief Executive	☐	☐
Director of Public Health/Public Health Consultant	☐	☐
Director of Finance	☐	☐
Director of Commissioning	☐	☐
Director of Performance Management	☐	☐
Director of Primary Care	☐	☐
Director of Information & Technology	☐	☐
Clinical Governance Lead	☐	☐
Clinical Governance Facilitator	☐	☐
Professional Advisers	☐	☐
Business Manager	☐	☐
Area Prescribing Committee	☐	☐
Health Technology Assessment Committee	☐	☐
Clinical Governance Committee	☐	☐
Clinical Audit Group	☐	☐
HImP/HIP Group	☐	☐
SaFF Group	☐	☐
Commissioning Team	☐	☐
Information Team	☐	☐
Board members	☐	☐
Lay representation	☐	☐

Title of Guidance document: _____

PRIMARY CARE ORGANISATIONS	Yes (✓)	No (✓)
Chief Executive	☐	☐
Professional Executive Committee	☐	☐
Board members	☐	☐
Clinical Governance Lead	☐	☐
Clinical Governance Facilitators	☐	☐
Clinical Governance Committee	☐	☐
GP Prescribing Lead	☐	☐
Professional Advisers	☐	☐
Nursing Lead	☐	☐
Prescribing Groups	☐	☐
Risk Management Lead	☐	☐
Primary Care Audit Group	☐	☐
Professional Representatives on PCO Board	☐	☐
Commissioning Lead	☐	☐
General Practitioners	☐	☐
Practice Pharmacists/Technicians	☐	☐
Practice Nurses	☐	☐
Practice Development Teams	☐	☐
Education and Training Leads	☐	☐
NHS Walk-in Centres	☐	☐
Lay representation	☐	☐

Title of Guidance document: _____

NHS TRUSTS	Yes (✓)	No (✓)
Chief Executive	☐	☐
Board members	☐	☐
Clinical Governance Lead	☐	☐
Clinical Governance Facilitators	☐	☐
Clinical Governance Committee	☐	☐
Clinical Guidelines Lead	☐	☐
Medical Director	☐	☐
Clinical Director (of relevant specialty)	☐	☐
Clinical Teams	☐	☐
Director of Nursing	☐	☐
Clinical Nurse Specialists	☐	☐
Chief Pharmacist	☐	☐
Directorate Pharmacists/Drug Information Pharmacists/Interface Pharmacists	☐	☐
PAMs	☐	☐
Director of Finance	☐	☐
Business Manager	☐	☐
Risk Management Leads	☐	☐
Drug & Therapeutics Committee	☐	☐
Clinical Audit Group	☐	☐
Clinical Effectiveness Group	☐	☐
Head of IM&T	☐	☐
Community Trusts – key individuals	☐	☐
District Nurses and Health Visitors	☐	☐
Lay representation	☐	☐

Title of Guidance document: _____

Additional expertise	Yes (✓)	No (✓)
Clinical Effectiveness Advisory Groups	☐	☐
Community Pharmacists	☐	☐
Practice Nurse Adviser	☐	☐
Practice Nurses Group	☐	☐
Practice Managers Group	☐	☐
Special Health Authorities, e.g. the National Blood Authority	☐	☐
Local Experts and Opinion Leaders	☐	☐
Dentists	☐	☐
Continuing Professional Development Leads	☐	☐
Education & Training Leads in PCOs	☐	☐
Postgraduate Educational Leads	☐	☐
District Medical Committee (DMC)	☐	☐
Local Medical Committee (LMC)	☐	☐
Local Pharmaceutical Committee (LPC)	☐	☐
Local Dental Committee (LDC)	☐	☐
Local Nursing & Midwifery Committee (LNMC)	☐	☐
Other local representative committees	☐	☐
NHS Direct and NHS Direct Wales	☐	☐
Local Authority	☐	☐
Social Services	☐	☐
Community Health Council (CHC)/Patient Advocacy and Liaison Services (PALS)	☐	☐
Patient/carer representation	☐	☐
Other lay representation	☐	☐

✓ **Questions which may help with planning for implementation of each piece of guidance**

Title of Guidance document: _____

	For action	
	Yes (✓)	**No** (✓)
Is it an issue?		
What is local current practice?	☐	☐
How does local current practice compare with regional/national trends?	☐	☐
Where, if any, is there a difference between current practice and what the guidance recommends?	☐	☐
Have we already looked at this? When did we look at this? Are the results/ conclusions still valid?	☐	☐
Has local Health Needs Assessment identified this area of care as a priority?	☐	☐
Is the guidance relevant to the local Health Improvement Programme?	☐	☐
What is the size of the issue locally, in terms of disease frequency, service configuration, treatment cost or potential savings?	☐	☐
What is the local expectation? Has there been widespread national publicity raising patient expectations of local service delivery?	☐	☐
Is there local information from OWAM, complaints or claims which indicate a different priority for this issue?	☐	☐
What are the implications?		
What would be the local impact of implementing the guidance? (e.g. on patients, workforce, services, resources, IM&T)	☐	☐

continued

Title of Guidance document: _____

	For action Yes (✓)	No (✓)
What are the financial implications of implementing the guidance?	☐	☐
Are there local contingency reserves for funding developments (e.g. specific reserves for NICE guidance) in-year?	☐	☐
How can adequate resources be identified?	☐	☐
What are the views of service users and local interested parties on this guidance?	☐	☐
Is there a corporate view of the guidance within and across professions locally?	☐	☐
Has there been adequate communication between neighbouring health authorities, trusts and PCOs to ensure co-ordinated decisions are made?	☐	☐

Verdict

How is implementation going to be achieved?	☐	☐
Has this decision been formally approved by the appropriate Board(s) or Committee(s)?	☐	☐
Can we facilitate the approach within the framework of clinical governance?	☐	☐

✓ **Examples of local resources/staff which may be affected by implementation of NICE guidance**

When looking at the resource implications of implementing any piece of guidance, also think about the effect on the following before developing an action plan. You may wish to brainstorm these issues locally.

Title of Guidance document: _____

Resources which may be affected	Yes (✓)	No (✓)
Drug budgets (PCO)	☐	☐
Drug budgets (Trust)	☐	☐
Other budgets (PCO)	☐	☐
Other budgets (Trust)	☐	☐
Waiting lists	☐	☐
Clinics	☐	☐
Referral guidance	☐	☐
Referral patterns	☐	☐
Community pharmacy (e.g. stocks/ordering)	☐	☐
PAMs	☐	☐
Staffing/workload implications	☐	☐
Accommodation	☐	☐
Equipment	☐	☐
Disinvestments in other services or technologies	☐	☐
Education and Training programmes	☐	☐

☑ Developing an action plan – examples of what to consider

Title of Guidance document: _____

Determine the responsibilities of each organisation	Consideration?	
	Yes (✓)	No (✓)

Define the specific roles of health authorities, PCOs and trusts. For example:

• **Responsibilities of the Health Authority**
  – determining who is responsible for developing the action plan
  – reviewing current practice
  – assessing financial, commissioning and resource implications
  – co-ordinating development and implementation of action plan
  – facilitating local dissemination of action plan
  – performance management of implementation of guidance
  – public health/HImP/HIP issues raised by guidance.
	☐	☐

• **Responsibilities of Trusts**
  – determining who is responsible for developing the action plan
  – reviewing current practice
  – assessing financial and resource implications
  – developing an action plan
  – internal sensitisation to, and dissemination of, action plan
  – implementing an action plan.
	☐	☐

continued

Title of Guidance document: _____

	Consideration?	
	Yes (✓)	No (✓)
● Responsibilities of PCOs	☐	☐
– determining who is responsible for developing the action plan		
– reviewing current practice		
– assessing financial, commissioning and resource implications		
– developing an action plan		
– internal sensitisation to, and dissemination of, action plan		
– implementing an action plan		
– integrating activities with local Trust(s) and neighbouring PCOs.		

Title of Guidance document: _____

Plan guidance implementation in clinical teams	Consideration?	
	Yes (✓)	No (✓)

Note: The term 'clinical team' is used to describe a unit, ward, directorate or department of a Trust, primary healthcare team, general (medical or dental) practice etc.

Structures: appoint Co-ordinators and Steering Groups

- Each team should have a named individual to co-ordinate guidance implementation within the clinical team. This person may be the Team Clinical Governance Lead and should be aware of national programmes such as that published by NICE. The Trust or PCO Clinical Governance Lead should know this person. Larger teams may need quality/clinical effectiveness groups to prioritise the timetable to implement guidelines. ☐ ☐

- Form an implementation steering group (this should be task-driven and goal-oriented and as small as is practical). In small teams this task may be delegated to an individual. Be aware of, and contact, other teams who will be responding to the guidance as well. ☐ ☐

Identify the area(s) of clinical practice involved ☐ ☐

Involve key stakeholders

- For each piece of guidance the co-ordinator or quality group should identify key stakeholders to agree an implementation policy. A standard policy that can be adopted for each piece of guidance might be helpful. ☐ ☐

continued

Title of Guidance document: _____

	Consideration?	
	Yes (✓)	**No** (✓)
• Identify who is to be involved (be wary of excluding people). Think of those who are directly involved, and those who may subsequently be affected by the change in practice.	☐	☐
• Identify who needs to be involved in making the changes.	☐	☐
• Who else outside your team needs to be informed or who may have something to contribute?	☐	☐

Raise awareness of the guidance

• Use email, photocopying, notices, team briefings, educational outreach etc. Encourage written comments and open discussion.	☐	☐

Establish baseline data

• Clarify current procedures and performance and then compare with the guidance. Ensure that data are collected which accurately reflect the current position, and provide a sound baseline for planning, monitoring progress and auditing outcomes.	☐	☐

Determine implementation approach

• Decide nature of implementation plan, taking account of current practice, local priorities and available resources.	☐	☐
• It may be that achieving full implementation involves a long-term commitment to change, and a shorter-term plan with partial implementation of	☐	☐

the guidance. To do this, those elements of the guidance that are already in place locally, and those that are not, should be identified. Any such process needs to be robust, with transparent systems for agreeing local implementation.

- Decisions to modify NICE guidance must be transparent and defensible if challenged. In these circumstances, it should be documented that the guidance has been considered and that there is a justifiable reason why alternative action has been taken. A reasonable test is whether such reasons could be justified in Court. ☐ ☐

- What changes are needed to current practice? (Detail them.) ☐ ☐

Define success criteria

- Define the indicators of a successful implementation. Test any suggested action against these performance indicators, to see how many would be moved in the right direction. ☐ ☐

Identify barriers to change

- Identify potential barriers and resistance to change and develop a plan to deal with them. ☐ ☐

- Identify 'leaders', 'innovators' etc. Also identify driving forces. ☐ ☐

- Will changes interfere with other activities already going on locally? ☐ ☐

Identify resources needed

- Resources will include finance, personnel and time, IM&T and other equipment. ☐ ☐

- Where can resources best be obtained from? ☐ ☐

continued

Title of Guidance document: _____

	Consideration?	
	Yes (✓)	No (✓)

Decide who will be responsible for managing information

- Decide how to get relevant information out to all key stakeholders, and identify one individual to collate and disseminate all information relating to each guideline. Disseminate widely a summary of the local impact of a guideline, and an implementation plan to those who need to take action. ☐ ☐

Identify mechanisms and networks for implementation

- Use existing mechanisms/networks for implementation rather than set up new ones, where possible. Ensure that the action plan is co-ordinated through existing clinical governance frameworks, as well as across primary and secondary care. ☐ ☐
- What mechanisms do you already have for dealing with the above? ☐ ☐
- You may find it helpful to consider the evidence on how to achieve change in clinical practice (*see* Further reading on pp. 37–8). ☐ ☐

Determine milestones with timescales

- How and by when will changes be made? ☐ ☐
- Set out timescales for each stage of the implementation process and establish review dates. (Set realistic targets.) ☐ ☐

Use information technology to facilitate implementation

- Consider the use of information technology, especially clinical support systems in primary and secondary care, for assisting in the implementation process. PRODIGY is a clinical decision support tool developed for use by GPs, and some guidance (including that produced by NICE) will be directly incorporated into it. Other clinical decision support tools are being developed in secondary care and specific guidance such as that produced by NICE should be incorporated wherever possible to assist in the implementation process.

Identify training and education needs

- Identify any training needs, e.g. if a new procedure is recommended and there is no local expertise, there may be a significant training and/or recruitment requirement before the new technology can be implemented locally. There may also be a need to include elements of the guidance in educational programmes for relevant professionals.

Consider the publicity aspects of guidance implementation

- Effective communication within teams, and with other teams, is essential for successful implementation. Consider how to publicise what your team is doing, what the expected outcomes and benefits are, and what is to be achieved.

continued

Title of Guidance document: _____

	Consideration?	
	Yes (✓)	**No** (✓)
• How will you best manage patients' expectations around each piece of guidance? Consider the use of patient information leaflets and proactive media statements.	☐	☐
• Keep all relevant people informed as to what is happening and why.	☐	☐

Incorporate guidance implementation into existing performance management systems locally

• The performance management of individuals and organisations should be linked to the successful implementation of the guidance.	☐	☐

Define methods for monitoring the implementation process

• These should include roles and responsibilities, achievement of milestones and success criteria. Regular evaluation dates should be set.	☐	☐
• Monitor the new outcomes – consider audit, patient feedback and team comments.	☐	☐
• Remember to look out for guidance revisions (see the NICE web site).	☐	☐
• Keep a written record of who was involved in the process and how it was undertaken.	☐	☐

Define audit methodologies for each guideline

- These may already be defined within the guidance document itself. ☐ ☐

Define feedback processes

- Include processes for feeding back any comments and results to Trusts, PCOs, HAs, Regional Office/NHS Wales and, ultimately, to the originating body itself (e.g. NICE). ☐ ☐
- Feedback from users and team members will be useful. ☐ ☐
- Encourage and remind team members about changes. Reward/acknowledge success. ☐ ☐
- Tell others about it – what went well and what didn't. ☐ ☐

Consider other key stakeholder interests

- Consider the role and potential impact on/of stakeholders, e.g. pharmaceutical and medical devices industries, patient/carer organisations, staff groupings, other agencies and other commercial concerns. Develop a process to best co-ordinate pharmaceutical industry and other commercial contacts and issues, and to obtain input from patient/carer organisations. ☐ ☐

Many of the ideas in this checklist were contributed by:
Dr Paul Myres, Primary Care Adviser, Clinical Effectiveness Support Unit (Wales) tmmpb@globalnet.co.uk

✔️ **An example checklist to support the process of guidance implementation in clinical teams**

Title of Guidance: _____

	Yes (✓)	No (✓)
Have we clearly identified the need for particular changes?	☐	☐
Have we clearly stated what we are trying to achieve?	☐	☐
Does this include the patient/carer perspective?	☐	☐
Are we prepared to challenge accepted behaviour and beliefs?	☐	☐
Do we know what the baseline position is now?	☐	☐
Do we understand our current processes?	☐	☐
Do we have local experts and peer opinion leaders on board?	☐	☐
Are all the key stakeholders involved/being consulted (including patients)?	☐	☐
Do we have dedicated project management?	☐	☐
Have we consulted the evidence on changing practice?	☐	☐
Do we have the necessary commitment across the locality?	☐	☐
Do we have a realistic action plan?	☐	☐
Have we identified the necessary resources?	☐	☐
Have we considered the potential barriers?	☐	☐
Have we identified strategies to overcome them?	☐	☐
Can we call on others for assistance?	☐	☐
Have we identified how the organisation and others will learn from the process?	☐	☐

Clinical Effectiveness Support Unit (Wales) – remit currently under review

Steps towards implementation – who could be involved at each stage?

These are the main steps which may be considered when national guidance is issued. At a local level some of these steps will be more or less relevant, depending on the nature of the guidance. These steps have been described in more detail in the main part of the handbook. Here, it may be useful to identify who in your organisation is responsible for, and which individuals or groups will be involved in, each step.

Title of Guidance document: _____

Step	Lead individual/ group	Other individuals/ groups involved
Overall responsibility for managing the implementation of this guidance		
Initiating implementation of the guidance		
Assessing resource implications of the guidance		
Developing an action plan		

continued

Title of Guidance document: _____

Step	Lead individual/ group	Other individuals/ groups involved
Implementation of the guidance – who should be involved?		
Developing a local approach to implementing the guidance		
Circulating the guidance and publicising action plans		
Identifying the best strategies for implementing the guidance		
Monitoring guidance implementation		
Evaluation and audit of guidance implementation		
Feedback		

☑ An example of a 'recommendation proforma' for implementing guidance

Title of NICE Guidance: _____

Date of meeting: _____

Lead person: _____

Guidance summary:

Local implications:

Recommendation:

Courtesy of STAMP (Stockport Technologies And Managed Prescribing)
Jan Hewitt, Director of Performance, Stockport Health Authority
jan.hewitt@stockport-ha.nwest.nhs.uk

✓ **Who has received guidance directly from NICE and who else needs to see it?**

These lists were compiled in brainstorming sessions during the development of this handbook. Please note that these lists are not exhaustive and that in different organisations titles may vary.

Title of Guidance document: _____

HEALTH AUTHORITY
Primary contact receiving the organisation's copies of each piece of NICE guidance: _____

Person responsible for onward dissemination: _____

	Received directly? (✓)	Needs to receive a copy? (✓)
Chief Executive	☐	☐
Director of Public Health	☐	☐
Director of Finance	☐	☐
Director of Commissioning	☐	☐
Director of Performance Management	☐	☐
Director of Primary Care	☐	☐
Director of Information & Technology	☐	☐
Clinical Governance Lead	☐	☐
Clinical Governance Facilitator	☐	☐
Public Health Consultants	☐	☐
Medical Adviser	☐	☐
Pharmaceutical Adviser	☐	☐
Other professional advisers	☐	☐

	Received directly? (✓)	Needs to receive a copy? (✓)
Business Manager	☐	☐
Area Prescribing Committee	☐	☐
Health Technology Assessment Committee	☐	☐
Clinical Governance Committee	☐	☐
Clinical Audit Group	☐	☐
HImP/HIP Group	☐	☐
SaFF Group	☐	☐
Commissioning Team	☐	☐
Information Team	☐	☐
Lay member	☐	☐

PRIMARY CARE ORGANISATIONS
Primary contact receiving the organisation's copies of each piece of NICE guidance: _____

Person responsible for onward dissemination: _____

	Received directly? (✓)	Needs to receive a copy? (✓)
Chief Executive	☐	☐
Professional Executive Committee	☐	☐
Clinical Governance Lead	☐	☐
Clinical Governance Facilitators	☐	☐
Clinical Governance Committee	☐	☐
GP Prescribing Lead	☐	☐
Prescribing Adviser	☐	☐
Commissioning Lead	☐	☐
Nursing Lead	☐	☐
PCO Board Members	☐	☐
General Practitioners	☐	☐
Practice Pharmacists/ Technicians	☐	☐
Practice Nurses	☐	☐
GP Practice Leads for Prescribing	☐	☐
Practice Development Teams	☐	☐
Education and Training Leads	☐	☐
Prescribing Groups	☐	☐
Risk Management Lead	☐	☐
Primary Care Audit Group	☐	☐
Lay member	☐	☐

NHS TRUSTS
Primary contact receiving the organisation's
copies of each piece of NICE guidance: _____

Person responsible for onward
dissemination: _____

	Received directly? (✓)	Needs to receive a copy? (✓)
Chief Executive	☐	☐
Clinical Governance Lead	☐	☐
Clinical Governance Facilitators	☐	☐
Medical Director	☐	☐
Clinical Director (of relevant specialty)	☐	☐
Consultants	☐	☐
Clinical Teams	☐	☐
Director of Nursing	☐	☐
Clinical Nurse Specialists	☐	☐
Chief Pharmacist	☐	☐
Directorate Clinical Pharmacists	☐	☐
Clinical Guidelines Lead	☐	☐
PAMs	☐	☐
Director of Finance	☐	☐
Business Manager	☐	☐
Risk Management Leads	☐	☐
Clinical Governance Committee	☐	☐
Drug & Therapeutics Committee	☐	☐
Clinical Audit Group	☐	☐
Clinical Effectiveness Group	☐	☐
Head of IM&T	☐	☐

continued

	Received directly? (✓)	Needs to receive a copy? (✓)
Community Trusts – key individuals	☐	☐
District Nurses and Health Visitors	☐	☐
Lay member	☐	☐

OTHERS
Person responsible for onward dissemination: _____

	Received directly? (✓)	Needs to receive a copy? (✓)
Clinical Effectiveness Advisory Groups	☐	☐
District Medical Committee (DMC)	☐	☐
Local Medical Committee (LMC)	☐	☐
Local Pharmaceutical Committee (LPC)	☐	☐
Local Dental Committee (LDC)	☐	☐
Local Nursing & Midwifery Committee (LNMC)	☐	☐
Other local representative committees	☐	☐
Local Experts and Opinion Leaders	☐	☐
NHS Walk-in Centres	☐	☐
Practice Nurse Adviser	☐	☐
Practice Nurses Group	☐	☐
Practice Managers Group	☐	☐
Community Pharmacists	☐	☐
Dentists	☐	☐
Continuing Professional Development Leads	☐	☐
Education & Training Leads in PCOs	☐	☐
Postgraduate Educational Leads	☐	☐
Local healthcare libraries and intranets	☐	☐

continued

	Received directly? (✓)	Needs to receive a copy? (✓)
NHS Direct and NHS Direct Wales	☐	☐
Local Authority	☐	☐
Social Services	☐	☐
Private Nursing Homes	☐	☐
Community Health Council (CHC)/Patient Advocacy and Liaison Services (PALS)	☐	☐
Patient/carer representation	☐	☐
Other lay representation	☐	☐

Tips for local circulation of NICE guidance

These ideas were compiled in brainstorming sessions during the development of this handbook.

Availability of NICE guidance

The first page of NICE technology appraisal guidance is designed to be photocopied and circulated. All the guidance is contained on this single page and the text is also available in Welsh. This page may be circulated to all relevant healthcare professionals and managers, whereas the full text may be disseminated to key stakeholders who have not already received it.

Copies of the A4 guidance can be ordered on 08701 555 455. NICE guidance is also published on their web site – visit the 'Publications' section of this site to download a PDF version.

Onward dissemination options

Ensure a named lead is responsible for local dissemination of each piece of guidance. Identify and use existing groups, e.g. Drug & Therapeutics Committee, Area Prescribing Committee, local professional committees, who may help take on the dissemination role.

Advertise the publication of new guidance at organisational briefings, educational meetings and in Board papers. Use email to inform people that the guidance is available. Copies of the guidance may be circulated via a local intranet, on a local web site or by CD ROM.

It is important that such information is updated if the guidance changes. Where possible, why not create a link to the relevant page of the NICE web site?

Internet training may be needed to ensure that healthcare professionals and managers are easily able to access the information promptly. Health authorities, trusts and PCOs should ensure appropriate access to the NHSnet and Internet by primary and secondary care staff.

Customisation

Presentation of the guidance may need to be further customised depending on the audience it is intended to reach, for example translation into other languages. Use newsletters and mailshots to further circulate the guidance.

NICE will prepare a version of its guidance for patients/ carers. This will explain the nature of the clinical recommendations, the implications for the standards that patients can expect, and the broad nature of the evidence on which the recommendations are based. This version could be used by the local media, and in liaison with patient/carer organisations. The text of this advice will always be appended to the main guidance document in order that it can be incorporated into local patient information leaflets.

NICE publish copies of press releases on their web site the same day they issue the guidance – feel free to adapt them to produce your own local press releases.

Some practical tips for implementing guidance and managing required change

The ideas below were suggested by the focus groups involved in the development of this handbook. These ideas have been grouped under the types of interventions that have been shown to change practice, as described in *Effective Health Care: getting evidence into practice*.

Interventions which change practice

Effective single interventions include educational outreach, patient-mediated interventions and reminders. The use of opinion leaders has mixed effects and should be used selectively.

Continuing professional development
- Educate healthcare professionals via postgraduate education programmes, GP trainers, personal & practice development plans, and continuing professional development schemes.
- Use multi-disciplinary education programmes where appropriate.
- Encourage self-review of clinical practice.
- Use peer pressure; identify local enthusiasts who can act as change agents, e.g. professional advisers, opinion leaders.
- Enlist local support to assist in the implementation process, e.g. professionals running disease management clinics, specialist nurses/technicians, community/practice/hospital pharmacists, administrative/IT support, quality assurance groups, e.g. MAAG, clinical effectiveness groups, PAMs, other contractors.

Dissemination
There is little evidence that passive dissemination alone results in behaviour change. However, this approach may be useful for raising awareness of messages. Dissemination by active educational interventions is more effective.

Interventions to improve clinical practice

Educational outreach approaches and ongoing feedback are generally effective. Feedback that includes specific recommendations is more likely to change behaviour than general feedback on current behaviour.

- Set up a programme of academic detailing, e.g. a 'NICE rep' to encourage adoption of specific guidance.

Audit and feedback

Peer comparison alone is unlikely to result in substantial quality improvement and may be inefficient. Audit and feedback can be effective in improving performance, in particular for prescribing and test ordering, although widespread use of audit and feedback is not supported by evidence.

- Provide support, motivation and encouragement. Professionals are bombarded with information and are in danger of developing 'guideline fatigue'.

Reminders (manual or computerised)

The use of computer-based decision support systems can lead to improvements in decisions (e.g. on drug dosage, the provision of preventative care, and the general clinical management of patients).

- Use markers and prompts in patient records to monitor progress.
- Include guidance in local primary and secondary care formularies, and care pathways. Revise local guidelines and prescribing strategies in the light of NICE guidance.
- Include in contracts with service providers.
- Include in audit contracts.
- Include in accountability frameworks.

Computerised information systems

Different information interventions, including provider and patient prompts, computer-assisted patient education and computer-assisted treatment planners, have improved care.

- Use information technology, e.g. PRODIGY, electronic prescribing in hospitals. Warning flags indicating the existence of NICE guidance could be included in eMIMS, eMeReC, PRODIGY, eBNF, eDTB, GP and hospital prescribing systems etc. NICE will use PRODIGY to disseminate their guidance but GPs need to be encouraged to use it as part of their every day practice. Any shortfalls in computerisation in GP surgeries and hospitals will need to be addressed for this approach to be widely successful.
- Include guidance in prescribing and equipment formularies, electronic and paper-based.
- Provide practical tools (aide memoire, risk calculator etc).

Media

Mass media campaigns have an effect on health services utilisation.

- Launch patient education campaigns.
- Involve patients and the community; having patient/carer organisations on your side can be helpful.
- Communicate widely the potential impact of implementation of the guidance.

Other suggestions

- Consider incentive schemes, or disincentives, relating to targets set by NICE, e.g. maximum doses of proton pump inhibitors prescribed. Incentives for change can include financial reward, resource reallocation, education and training, performance feedback and empowerment. Programmes involving incentives should be agreed locally, as purely 'top down' schemes can undermine full participation.
- Provide adequate resources (time, money, disinvestments elsewhere) to implement the guidance.
- Maintain the momentum of any intervention process.

Further reading

Effective Health Care: getting evidence into practice. NHS Centre for Reviews and Dissemination. February 1999, Volume 5, Number 1.

☑ An example template for monitoring the implementation process

Title of Guidance document: _____

Organisation: _____

Key recommendations   1
from the guidance: 2
              3

Action	Responsible individual or group	Target date	Details of current progress	Achieved (date)/ comments
Initiating implementation				
Assessing resource implications				
Developing an action plan				
Circulating guidance and publicising action plan				
Implementing guidance				
Evaluation and audit of implementation				
Feedback				

✓ Examples of data sources available for use in monitoring, audit and evaluation

Title of Guidance document: _____

	To be used in the audit of this guidance? (✓)
PRIMIS/MIQUEST	☐
GP computer data	☐
PACT/PARC data	☐
Prescribing Toolkit data	☐
Local regional databases, e.g. West Midlands GPRD	☐
Hospital information systems	☐
Hospital prescribing data	☐
Community pharmacy	☐
Public health morbidity data	☐
Outcome data	☐
Results of previous audits	☐
Patient satisfaction surveys	☐
Patient panels	☐
Complaints	☐
Critical incident data	☐

☑ An example template for feeding back the results of guidance implementation at Board level

---

Title of Guidance document: _____

Date of issue: _____

Date of initial review: _____

Action agreed:

Date of post-implementation review(s): _____

Action required to address any problems with the implementation:

Evaluation date(s): _____

Monitoring/Evaluation/Audit/Feedback:

Adapted from STAMP (Stockport Technologies And Managed Prescribing)
Jan Hewitt, Director of Performance, Stockport Health Authority
jan.hewitt@stockport-ha.nwest.nhs.uk

Useful web sites

Association of British Health Care Industries (www. abhi.org.uk)

Bandolier (www.jr2.ox.ac.uk/bandolier)

British Association of Medical Managers (www.bamm. co.uk)

British National Formulary (www.bnf.org)

Clinical Effectiveness Support Unit (Wales) (CESU) (www.cesu.wales.nhs.uk)

Clinical Evidence (BMJ) (www.clinicalevidence.org)

Clinical Governance Research & Development Unit (www.le.ac.uk/cgrdu)

Cochrane Database (www.update-software.com/cochrane/ cochrane-frame.html)

Cochrane EPOC (Effective Practice and Organisation of Care) Group (www.abdn.ac.uk/hsru/epoc)

Commission for Health Improvement (www.chi.nhs.uk)

Department of Health (www.doh.gov.uk)

Health Evidence Bulletins Wales (www.uwcm.ac.uk/uwcm/ lb/pep)

Health Technology Assessment (www.hta.nhsweb.nhs.uk)

Information and IT for the NHS (www.doh.gov.uk/ nhsexipu/index.htm)

National Assembly for Wales – Health of Wales Information Service (www.wales.gov.uk/subihealth/index.htm)

National Association of Primary Care (www.primarycare. co.uk)

National Institute for Clinical Excellence (www.nice. org.uk)

National Prescribing Centre (www.npc.co.uk (Internet) and nww.npc.ppa.nhs.uk (NHSnet))

National Service Frameworks (www.doh.gov.uk/nsf/ nsfhome.htm)

NHS Centre for Reviews and Dissemination (University of York) (www.york.ac.uk/inst/crd)

NHS Confederation (www.nhsconfed.net)

NHS IM&T Electronic Library (www.standards.nhsia.nhs.uk/library/)

NHS Learning Zone (www.doh.gov.uk/learningzone/menu.htm)

Pathways to NSFs (www.nsfpathways.co.uk)

Prescription Pricing Authority (www.ppa.org.uk)

Primary Care National Electronic Library for Health (www.nelh-pc.nhs.uk)

PRIMIS/MIQUEST (www.clinical-info.co.uk/index.htm)

PRODIGY (www.prodigy.nhs.uk)

Regional Medicines Information Centres' outputs (www.ukdipg.org.uk, www.druginfozone.org)

SCHARR (University of Sheffield School of Health and Related Research) (www.shef.ac.uk/~scharr/about.htm)

Turning Research into Practice (TRIP) (www.tripdatabasc.com)

Appendix 2
Practical examples

How different organisations are delegating responsibility
    for NICE guidance   93
Initiating implementation   95
Assessing the resource implications of guidance   99
How different organisations have developed their
    action plans   101
Who is being involved in the implementation of
    NICE guidance?   105
How NICE guidance is being circulated locally   107
Monitoring guidance implementation   112

How different organisations are delegating responsibility for NICE guidance

In **Birmingham Health Authority**, a Directorate of Policy Analysis is, in part, responsible for accepting and interpreting national, regional and other guidance, particularly in relation to identifying funding opportunities. The model has worked well and the Health Authority is establishing a small group to receive and implement NICE and other guidance in a similar way.

This will draw on expertise from finance, public health, commissioning and the pharmaceutical adviser. Output from the group will be for local consumption and recommendations will be made to the HA Board and via the PCO management route. The function of this group will be not only to deal with NICE guidance but also to advise on the introduction of medicines and technologies not covered by NICE.

Peter Spilsbury, Director of Healthcare Services, Birmingham Health Authority

Within **Hammersmith Hospitals NHS Trust**, individual clinical directorates are expected to lead on NICE guidance for their clinical areas. For example, the lead clinician for gastro-enterology has been charged with ensuring compliance with the proton pump inhibitor guidance and is working to audit current practice. The feedback mechanism is via clinical governance structures within the Directorate of Medicine. Guidance will go to the Drug & Therapeutics Committee for information.

The taxane guidance was in line with the New Drugs Panel's earlier decisions, and hence required no action. Had any action been necessary, the New Drugs Panel would have had to note and ratify any change in use required to bring the Trust in line with NICE guidance, and Cancer Services would then be required to enact any change.

The Trust is managed very clearly through the directorate structure and service developments are put forward by each directorate for compiling into the Trust business plan, and for onward funding consideration by the Health Authority. All actions arising from NICE will be sent through the directorate structures for consideration with all other service pressures and developments, as are other external influences such as Controls Assurance, Royal College visits etc. Requests for additional funding that cannot be met within Trust resources go to the Health Authority Priority Setting Subcommittee, which prioritises all requests for funding allocation each year as and when monies become available.

Ann Jacklin, Chief Pharmacist, Hammersmith Hospitals NHS Trust
(ajacklin@hhnt.org)

Initiating implementation

The **Barnet, Enfield & Haringey Health Authority** Executive Strategy Group will have overall responsibility for determining the likely impact of each piece of NICE guidance and will co-ordinate any action to be taken to assess the impact, e.g. in terms of the number of patients likely to be affected, the broad implications for primary care and local secondary care, and the likely cost implications to be fed into the HImP/HIP and SaFF processes.

The Executive Strategy Group will identify a lead person to take forward the above work for each guideline. The lead will liaise with relevant Trusts and PCOs. The lead will be encouraged to identify an existing group to work with wherever possible, rather than set up a new group. The Public Health and Information Departments of Barnet, Enfield & Haringey Health Authority will work together to assess the projected numbers of patients likely to be affected.

For some of the guidance the Clinical Effectiveness Review Group may consider the evidence of effectiveness on which NICE guidance is based, in order to advise the Executive Strategy Group in detail. The whole process, from publication of the guidance to the decision of the Executive Strategy Group, should not take longer than three months.

Mike Beaman, Pharmaceutical Adviser, Barnet, Enfield & Haringey Health Authority
(mike.beaman@barnet-ha.nthames.nhs.uk)

In **Oxfordshire Health Authority** there is a multi-disciplinary forum chaired by the Director of Public Health. This forum is responsible for making priority decisions on a number of issues, including prescribing of some drugs. When this forum – known as the Priorities Forum – has agreed its recommendations, these are formulated into 'Lavender Statements' which are then widely distributed to GPs and Trusts. They appear to be highly regarded by most and are used by GPs to reinforce their messages to patients. Examples include the use of NHS-funded transport in non-emergency situations:

PRIORITIES FORUM POLICY STATEMENT

NUMBER: 31

SUBJECT: Eligibility for NHS-funded transport for Oxfordshire patients in non-emergency situations

DATE OF DECISION/MEETING: 17 February 2000

EXPLANATORY NOTE: NHS-funded transport for essential non-emergency journeys is arranged through the Oxfordshire Ambulance Service. As there have recently been severe problems in making this transport available to patients needing it, this policy statement has been produced to reiterate the principles and guidelines contained in a locally-agreed NHS transport purchasing document of early 1998. It is thought that these may not so far have been applied consistently in Oxfordshire.

POLICY

Oxfordshire Health Authority will only fund NHS transport for patients who need to make essential journeys in situations that are not medical emergencies if the patients fulfill one of the following criteria:

1 They need skilled assistance to transfer them to and from a vehicle.
2 Their disability or medical need, or the nature of their treatment programme, makes it impossible, difficult or undesirable for them to have to make their own travel arrangements, either by public or by private transport.

Patients who are able to walk independently are not, therefore, in general likely to qualify for NHS transport. They may do so, however, if their condition, physical or mental, could result in a risk of embarrassment to themselves or others, including an inability to comply with hospital-based treatment, if they undertake the journey independently.

They may also qualify if:

1 The journey is necessary for the regular use by them of time-scheduled medical equipment or resources and an accurate time of arrival is only likely to be possible through the use of NHS transport.

2 They live in a rural area remote from suitable public transport and are unable to make their own private transport arrangements.

Escorts

Requests for escorts for patients having NHS non-emergency transport will not be considered unless:

1 The patient is under 18 years of age.
2 The patient requires the additional assistance of the escort during the journey or treatment as a direct result of his/her medical need, disability or mental health condition.

Jane Harrison, Clinical Effectiveness Co-coordinator, Oxfordshire Health Authority
(jane.harrison@oxon-ha.anglox.nhs.uk)

In **Plymouth Community Services Trust** a '5 question letter' (*see* below), compatible with that of neighbouring Trusts, is sent out every time new national guidance is published. This provides the Trust with an audit trail of what new changes in practice are occurring as a result of recommendations.

DATE

Dear Colleague,

I am pleased to enclose the latest recommendations relating to your service.

In order to ensure national recommendations are implemented we need to confirm what action has been taken as a result of these recommendations. In order to do this I would greatly appreciate you responding to the following questions:

- Does the conclusion raise any issues for practice within the Trust?

- Are the recommendations contained with this document compatible with your current practice?

- If not, will you be changing your practice to meet these recommendations?

- If you will be changing your practice, please describe what the change will entail (and include resource implications if appropriate).

- If you will not be changing your practice, please state why.

If you do not think you are the most appropriate person to give a response to this letter, please inform me as soon as possible with another name.

It may be helpful to discuss this with colleagues in your specialist area before completing this response.

Further copies of this report have been sent to:

Please send me your response by:

Yours faithfully

Clinical Governance Manager

There is a feeling that new guidance will lead to dramatic changes in practice. This is usually not the case – so far most of the recommendations are based on long-standing evidence which up-to-date health professionals have long ago implemented. The beauty of this (5 question letter) approach is:

- it reassures people that they are really doing the right thing, and
- it enables practice to be standardised – a sort of rubber stamping of approval.

Where a dissent from practice is identified, it allows for a rationale to be recorded, and the Trust Board is then informed (via the relevant director).

Mary McClarey, Clinical Governance Manager, Plymouth Primary Care Trust
(mcclareym@netscapeonline.co.uk)

Assessing the resource implications of guidance

In **North & East Devon Health Authority**, a process has been developed which provides a standard mechanism for dealing with new drugs. It allows proper consideration and evaluation against other competing priorities before significant additional resources are committed. (*See* the algorithm.)

NICE recommendations join the process at the point of DPH evaluation. The DPH then decides the most appropriate course of action and oversees the production of a business case for evaluation by the Directors of Finance and final decision by the HImP Board. The Directors of Finance provide the professional evaluation of the business aspects of the case, ensuring that the financial analysis is robust and that wider service implications have been properly considered. They then make recommendations to the HImP Board.

The HImP Board confirms consistency with the HImP and considers funding implications against other competing priorities. A decision to approve may, for example, be to fund for introduction in-year, thus creating a call on the risk pool, or to defer until the following financial year when costs can be built in to the Service and Financial Framework.

Marilyn Ramsden, Chief Pharmaceutical Adviser, North & East Devon Health Authority
(marilyn.ramsden@nedevon-ha.swest.nhs.uk)

North & East Devon HA (NEDHA) Algorithm

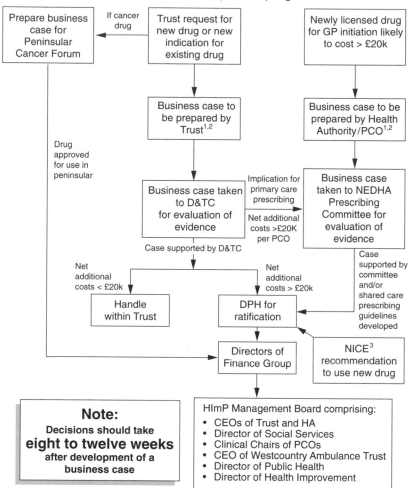

Note:

Decisions should take **eight to twelve weeks** after development of a business case

HImP Management Board comprising:
- CEOs of Trust and HA
- Director of Social Services
- Clinical Chairs of PCOs
- CEO of Westcountry Ambulance Trust
- Director of Public Health
- Director of Health Improvement

---

1   As a minimum, business cases must include:
- Clinical case for drug based on an independent evaluation of evidence
- Part year and full year costs
- Impact on other health services.

2   If a new drug replaces an existing formulary drug and releases a net saving, the Trust may agree that part of the net saving may be kept, for agreed developments within the Directorate sponsoring the drug.

3   The cost implications of any NICE recommendations will be assessed by the DPH. The Prescribing Committee will be consulted if a Shared Care Prescribing Guideline is thought to be needed.

How different organisations have developed their action plans

The following is the proposed process for the implementation of NICE guidance in **Bromley**. The Clinical Governance Forum (PCO Clinical Governance Leads, Trust Medical Directors, Director of Public Health) will oversee the implementation of NICE guidance.

In advance of NICE guidance being published:
- Establish with the Clinical Governance Forum and local representative committees if the guidance is relevant to them, under what circumstances and who is the lead person managerially and clinically.
- Response time to be within one week.
- Call first meeting of named leads or identified stakeholders (implementation group).
- Discuss issues and identify other stakeholders not included so far. Communication with external stakeholders and tertiary centres to be undertaken.
- Implementation group to agree baseline information requirements and timetable.

Once NICE guidance is published:
- Local policy formulated by implementation committee and/or Public Health.
- Policy will include present situation, situation following guidance and proposed implementation process.
- Proposals to be costed and other information such as staffing, training and development requirements also considered.
- Action plan to be formulated to change practice in line with recommendations, with timescales and milestones attached.
- Draft action plan shared with all relevant organisations.
- Final proposals agreed and all relevant chief executives or chairs of local representative committees to sign a formal commitment.
- Implementation group to consider what information should be provided to the press. Positive press statements to be issued wherever possible.

Implementation process:
To be undertaken by relevant agencies.

Monitoring:
Review process to be agreed as part of the implementation plan, with appropriate timescales and processes identified. Positive press statements to be issued wherever possible.

Andrew Scott-Clark, Pharmaceutical Adviser, Bexley, Bromley & Greenwich Health Authority
(andrew.scott-clark@bromley-ha.sthames.nhs.uk)

Bro Morgannwg Trust in Wales has developed a draft policy for dealing with NICE guidance, National Service Frameworks and other guidelines and protocols of similar importance.

- Guidance is received and registered within the Medical Director's department.
- The Medical Director decides the relevance for the Trust's directorates and departments.
- The existence of the guidance is reported to the Trust's Management Executive Committee and the Clinical Governance Sub-Committee of the Trust Board, and the Clinical Audit/ Effectiveness Committee. If necessary, it will be reported to other sub-committees such as Prescribing Strategy or Infection Control.
- The documentation is distributed to the appropriate Directors, who are asked to:

  - evaluate their performance against the guidance
  - consider an action plan required to achieve the standard set out in the guidance
  - ensure that the Directorate's Finance Officer is aware of the guidance and is involved in assessing costs/substitution costs to comply with the guidance, and any other financial implications there will be
  - if the need for new resources is identified, prepare a case to be put before the Health Authority
  - assess training and continuing professional development consequences.

- The Directorate reports back to the Management Executive Committee.
- The Management Executive Committee reports to the Clinical Governance Sub-Committee of the Trust Board.

Nicola John, Director of Pharmaceutical Public Health, Iechyd Morgannwg Health Authority
(nicola.john@morgannwg-ha.wales.nhs.uk)

At **Addenbrooke's NHS Trust** in Cambridge, the following process is used for implementing NICE guidance (see overleaf).

Fiona Ritchie, Head of Clinical Governance & Performance Review, Addenbrooke's NHS Trust
(fiona.ritchie@addenbrookes.nhs.uk)

NICE guidance implementation process (July 2000)

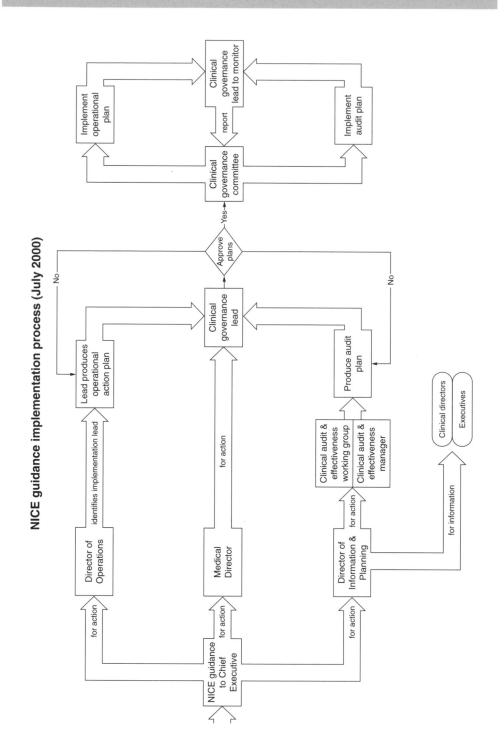

Who is being involved in the implementation of NICE guidance?

STAMP (Stockport Technologies And Managed Prescribing) Forum covers primary and secondary care within the **Stockport Health Authority** area, where all agencies are co-terminous. All NICE guidance is assessed and action agreed by this group. Its membership is:

- Health Authority – Chief Executive, Head of Health Service Development, Medical Adviser, Director of Public Health, Pharmaceutical Adviser, Clinical Governance Lead, Consultant in Public Health Medicine, New Technologies Lead.
- PCO Prescribing Leads.
- Trust Clinical Director and Medical Director.
- LMC and LPC representative.
- Public representative.
- Tertiary clinician.
- Social Services representative.

The following figure shows how STAMP interacts with other groups and organisations to ensure a unified approach to NICE guidance:

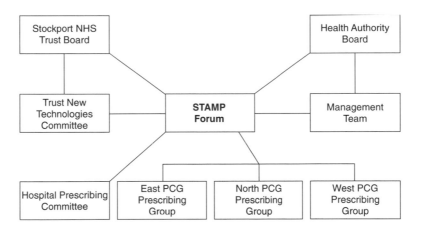

Jan Hewitt, Director of Performance, Stockport Health Authority (jan.hewitt@stockport-ha.nwest.nhs.uk)

In **Manchester**, NICE recommendations are on the agenda of the Area Prescribing Committee or Prescribing Strategy Group (PSG). This is to ensure awareness of the guidance (the group includes Trust representation) and to ensure compliance with guidance as part of the Health Authority's performance management role. This will also ensure that current policies reflect NICE guidance. The PSG issues city-wide guidance to GP practices and the prescribing leads within PCOs. This can then become part of the commissioning process via PCO prescribing sub-groups, which are sub-committees of the clinical governance committees. The process is as follows:

- NICE guidance is issued.
- PSG considers action required.
- Hospital Drug & Therapeutics Committees ensure guidance is implemented in secondary care in line with these recommendations.
- Prescribing sub-committees of PCOs ensure guidance to primary care is in line with these national recommendations and that commissioning arrangements are in line with the recommendations.
- Monitoring arrangements for the uptake of the guidance are followed through performance management arrangements, with evidence of monitoring and compliance requested under clinical governance arrangements.

Service developments within the PCOs are considered by commissioning and finance leads along with organisational chief executives. A finance representative sits on the prescribing sub-groups of the PCOs, and also on the Drug & Therapeutics Committees at all the hospital Trusts.

Melanie Ogden, Pharmaceutical Adviser, Manchester Health Authority
(ogdenm@manchester-ha.nwest.nhs.uk)

How NICE guidance is being circulated locally

The following is a suggested process from **Leeds** for the circulation of information concerning NICE guidance to key stakeholders within a Trust, undertaken by the Head of Pharmacy:

- Write a letter to key individuals inviting them to attend briefing sessions and enclosing a copy of the briefing material.
- Hold briefing sessions over lunchtime, supported by a buffet lunch, using a process of nominated deputies for those unable to attend.
- Email the guidance to a general audience across the Trust.
- Use existing newsletters circulated to professionals from the Drug & Therapeutics Committee.
- Use journal clubs and other education and training sessions.

This could enable about 50% of key stakeholders in the Trust to be reached. The remaining options would be to contact each individually by telephone or through an individual appointment. This could be undertaken by clinical staff should the message be sufficiently important.

Liz Kay, Head of Pharmacy Services, Leeds Teaching Hospitals NHS Trust
(eak@smtpgate.ulth.northy.nhs.uk)

A dissemination protocol for clinical practice documents, including NICE guidance, has been developed in **Leeds**:

Objective	Action	Responsibility
The well co-ordinated dissemination of key documents.	As relevant documents arrive in the Trust, pass them to the Knowledge Manager.	Directors.
The development of a well-informed initial distribution list.	Include the following in each distribution: – Lead clinicians for clinical governance – Chair of Clinical Governance Committee – Libraries – Clinical audit support team. Consult with lead clinical governance clinicians to add to list lead clinicians from the professions, opinion leaders and managers.	Knowledge Manager (KM). KM, in consultation with lead clinicians and local specialists.
The identification of local accountability arrangements for any implementation issues arising.	Identify any individuals or groups with a lead responsibility to respond to the document.	KM, in consultation with lead clinicians, directors and local specialists.
The identification of recent data on complaints, incidents and claims which might influence the Trust's implementation plan.	Identify any local risk management issues associated with the area featured in the paper.	KM, in consultation with the Risk Manager.
Recipients to understand the full context of the information.	Send the information along with an attached sheet detailing: – source – distribution list – local arrangements for responding to the document – local risk factors which may affect the relevance of the paper – any expectations on the recipients.	KM

Objective	Action	Responsibility
The Trust to develop an understanding of the effectiveness of its dissemination, and the needs of staff in relation to the information sent.	Send under the same cover as the information a questionnaire based on the format following this protocol.	KM
Prompt dissemination of clinical practice information.	Distribution to occur within 20 days of issue from source.	KM

Questions to be included under the same cover as the preceding information:

Title of document: _____

Name: _____

On what date did you read this document?

Who did you receive it from?

Had you already received it from anywhere else? If so, where?

Please rate the information in terms of its:
– clarity of presentation (1–10)
– relevance to your area of responsibility (1–10)
– quality of evidence (1–10)

How great are the implications of this paper, in terms of the need to change practice locally, for your area of responsibility? (1–10)

What action do you propose to take in response to reading this?
☐ None
☐ Distribute to colleagues (who, how many?)
☐ Make contact with the forum/person with lead responsibility for response to this document
☐ Seek support to critically appraise or understand its relevance to your area of responsibility
☐ Other (please state)

Are there any key people we have missed off the distribution list?

Additional comments:

Peter McGinnis, Director of Nursing and Quality, Leeds Community and Mental Health Services NHS Trust (petermcginnis@cwcom.net)

The Clinical Effectiveness Department at **Nottingham City Hospital NHS Trust** has developed an intranet web site which is being used to disseminate NICE guidance. The site provides links directly to each piece of guidance on the NICE web site and also includes details of the Trust's audit plans and hospital-wide or cross-town projects. The site will shortly be on the hospital's internet site.

Simon Castle, Clinical Effectiveness Co-ordinator, Nottingham City Hospital NHS Trust
(scastle@ncht.org.uk)

In **Liverpool**, the four PCG Prescribing Advisers collaborate when disseminating guidance and advice. Summaries of NICE guidance are circulated to all GPs on a single side of A4. The Liverpool PCG advisers have an informal group that meets once a month and are in contact by email. When new guidance is issued, a first draft paper is prepared, which is then circulated for comment before the final version is disseminated.

An email contact group for prescribing advisers in Mersey has been set up. The idea is to share guidance sent out to GPs, rather than each re-inventing the wheel. The long-term aim is to set up a web site to collate such guidance.

Although mailing guidance to GPs does not in itself result in successful implementation, it is an important first stage in the process. Favourable comments about this process have already been received, suggesting that the exercise is helpful.

Peter Johnstone, Prescribing Adviser, Octagon PCG/Alt Valley PCG, Liverpool
(peter.johnstone@liverpool-ha.nhs.uk)

Monitoring guidance implementation

In **Sefton**, the Director of Public Health convenes a small working group to provide advice on action for NICE guidance. Progress on NICE guidance implementation is reported to Sefton Clinical Governance Forum six-monthly and through to the Health Authority in the Annual Report. The following template is used to record action, milestones and progress for each piece of guidance:

NICE Guidance Action Plan

NICE Guideline: _____

Date: _____   Review date: _____

	Action	Rationale	Deadline	Progress report
PCG:				
HA:				
Trust:				
Advisory Committee:				
Other:				

Membership of Action Planning Group:

Paul Clark, Prescribing Support Pharmacist for West Lancashire PCG, and Primary Care Pharmacist for St Helens South PCG (clarkie@gofree.co.uk)

Appendix 3

What is NICE? What is the NPC?

What is CHI?

What is NICE?

NICE – The National Institute for Clinical Excellence – was set up as a Special Health Authority for England and Wales on 1 April 1999. Its role is to provide patients, health professionals and the public with authoritative, robust and reliable guidance on current 'best practice'. This guidance will consider both clinical and cost effectiveness.

NICE provides several types of guidance, including:

- Technology appraisals of new and existing health technologies.
- Clinical guidelines for the management of specific conditions.
- Referral advice for GPs.
- Clinical audit methods to support the technology appraisals and clinical guidelines.

NICE guidance

What is it?

Clinical guidelines and appraisals are systematically developed statements to help health professionals and patients make the best decisions about the most appropriate healthcare in particular circumstances. Research has shown that properly developed guidelines can lead to better patient care in practice. They sit alongside, and do not replace, the knowledge and skills of experienced health professionals. NICE is developing clear clinical guidelines to help health professionals give their patients the best care the NHS can afford.

NICE will make sure that its guidelines are based on robust research findings, are cost effective as well as clinically effective, and are communicated to clinicians and patients in a form that is useful on a day-to-day basis.

How is it developed?

NICE guidance is based on the best available research evidence and expert professional advice. They take into account both clinical effectiveness and cost effectiveness, and must be practical and affordable. In developing guidelines, NICE involves the clinical professions, the NHS, those who speak for patients and, of course, the relevant commercial enterprises.

NICE guidance may be developed from existing clinical guidelines prepared by others, if they fulfil the NICE criteria for quality and content, or NICE may commission the development of guidelines from scratch. Research may be commissioned by NICE, or consist of reviewing existing material. NICE may also produce advice about when patients should be referred from GPs to specialist care.

Why is it needed?

Some of the clinical guidelines, produced by independent groups or professional bodies, have been shown to be useful and effective. But others have potential bias or are of unacceptable or indeterminate quality. There has been no clear way of knowing into which category the guidelines you have in front of you fall, and no easy way of getting effective guidelines into practice across the country.

Partly as a result of this, there are unacceptable variations in the quality of care available for different patients in different parts of the country (so-called post-code healthcare). The Government is determined that this shall change, in order to equitably provide a genuinely National Health Service with dependable high standards of treatment wherever a patient lives.

National guidance, based on reliable evidence, is an essential part of achieving this. NICE will help to clarify, both for patients and professionals, which treatments work best for which patients, and which do not.

For more information about the work of NICE, please visit their website at www.nice.org.uk.

What is the National Prescribing Centre?

The National Prescribing Centre (NPC) is a health service organisation, formed in April 1996 by the Department of Health following a review of centrally funded support for prescribing and medicine use. Its aim is to:

'facilitate the promotion of high quality, cost-effective prescribing and medicines management through a co-ordinated and prioritised programme of activities aimed at supporting all relevant professionals and senior managers working in the modern NHS.'

The NPC delivers a broad range of activities across the following main areas of work:

- Information on medicines.
- Training and education.
- Dissemination of good practice.

In addition, the NPC considers how development of the following areas of activity, nationally, can be best informed in relation to prescribing:

- Information technology.
- Research and development.

The NPC has collaborative links with a wide range of relevant national bodies and professional groups. Part of the work of the NPC now comes under the NICE umbrella and we will be working increasingly closely with, and for, NICE over the coming years on effective information provision. The NPC is involved in the development of this handbook for a number of reasons:

- Because of the close working relationship now established with NICE.
- Because medicines use will play a key role in many of NICE's outputs.
- Because we have a strong track record in developing and delivering concise guides and resource documents for the

NHS. For example: *GP Prescribing Support*, September 1998; *Practical Clinical Governance in Primary Care: Audit Handbook*, April 2000; *Area Prescribing Committees: A Guide to Good Practice*, September 2000.

As a result of the above we have developed significant expertise in producing this type of publication and have created excellent networks with a wide range of key NHS personnel, who will be crucial to the implementation process for NICE guidance. A strong reputation for the quality and independence of our work has developed and this is also an important factor in our involvement.

For more information on the work and publications of the NPC please contact us on 0151 794 8134 or visit our web sites at www.npc.co.uk (Internet) and nww.npc.ppa.nhs.uk (NHSnet).

What is the Commission for Health Improvement?

The Commission for Health Improvement (CHI) is one part of a far reaching NHS reform programme to ensure that patients get the best possible care, no matter who they are, where they are or when they need it. Its aim is to help the NHS in England and Wales assure, monitor and improve the quality of patient care.

CHI began its work programme in April 2000, and over time will develop considerable knowledge, understanding and expertise to help NHS staff and organisations improve their services. Operating at arm's length from the Government, CHI will provide independent reassurance to patients that effective systems are in place to deliver high-quality services throughout the NHS.

CHI has four main areas of work, and these fall into the following areas:

- **Review** – CHI visits every NHS Trust and Health Authority (encompassing every PCO in England and LHG in Wales) every four years to help ensure that effective systems to continuously improve patient care are in place. CHI will assist these organisations, acknowledge and develop best practice and identify areas for improvement.
- **Investigate** – CHI responds to requests from individuals, organisations and the Secretary of State for Health or the National Assembly for Wales, where serious concerns are raised about the quality of services within an NHS organisation.
- **Studies** – CHI monitors the progress that the NHS is making towards meeting recommendations laid down by both National Service Frameworks and NICE guidance. The first study is a review of cancer services that will be published in summer 2001.
- **Leadership** – CHI will lead, review and assist NHS healthcare improvement and act as an adviser on best practice and problem solving. By reviewing clinical governance in every identified NHS organisation in England and Wales over the next four years, CHI is in a powerful position for the dissemination of good practice.

Appendix 4
Focus group members and
other acknowledgements

Focus group members

Individuals with a wide range of roles and experience were invited to take part in the focus groups. The list below reflects those who were able to attend.

Helen Allanson
Pharmaceutical Adviser, South Lancashire Health Authority

David Allegranza
Public Health Specialist, Avon Health Authority

Alison Astles
PCG Pharmaceutical Adviser, Bootle & Litherland PCG

Nigel Barnes
Pharmaceutical Adviser, Walsall Health Authority

Beryl Bevan
Prescribing Manager, Ealing, Hammersmith & Hounslow Health Authority

Alex Bower
Head of Pharmacy, Wakefield Health Authority

Steve Brown
Director of Pharmacy Services, Bristol Royal Infirmary

Jane Brown
PCG Pharmaceutical Adviser, Cheltenham & Tewkesbury PCG

Paul Brown
Pharmaceutical Adviser, Tees Health Authority

Peter Burrill
Chief Pharmaceutical Adviser, North Derbyshire Health Authority

Sonia Colwill
Principal Pharmaceutical Adviser, Lambeth, Southwark & Lewisham Health Authority

Liz Corteville
PCG Lead Prescribing Adviser, West Southampton & Test Valley South PCG

Dr Sue Davies
Medical Adviser, Somerset Health Authority

Stephen Deitch
Pharmaceutical Adviser, Hillingdon Health Authority

Amalin Dutt
Pharmaceutical Adviser, Camden & Islington Health Authority

Margaret Edwards
Community Nurse Lecturer, King's College, London

Elizabeth Evans
Clinical Governance Lead, Monmouthshire LHG

Gruff Evans
Clinical Governance Lead, Denbighshire LHG

Alison Ewing
Chief Pharmaceutical Officer, Countess of Chester Hospital NHS Trust

Lee Furniss
PCG Liaison Pharmacist, North Islington PCG

Colin Gidman
Pharmaceutical Adviser, North Cheshire Health Authority

Susan Grieve
PCG Pharmaceutical Adviser, High Weald PCG

Dr Bill Gutteridge
Consultant in Public Health/Primary Care, Hillingdon Health
Authority

Fiona Harris
Pharmaceutical Adviser, North & Mid-Hampshire Health
Authority

Dr John Haworth
Medical Adviser, East Lancashire Health Authority

Karen Homan
Pharmaceutical Adviser, Bedfordshire Health Authority

Helen Hulme
PCG Prescribing Adviser, South Amber Valley PCG

Ann Jacklin
Chief Pharmacist, Hammersmith Hospitals NHS Trust

Dr Jennifer Kay
PCG Clinical Governance Lead, Enfield Southgate PCG

Helen Liddell
Pharmaceutical Adviser, Rotherham Health Authority

Huw Lloyd
Clinical Governance Lead, Conwy LHG

Andrea Loudon
Pharmaceutical Adviser, Morecambe Bay Health Authority

Sue Lunec
PCG Prescribing Support Pharmacist, Redditch PCG

Rachel Marsden
Prescribing Adviser, Newport LHG

Peter Matthews
Pharmaceutical Adviser, Sandwell Health Authority

Dr Nina Moorman
PCG Prescribing Lead, Bristol West PCG

Dr George Moses
PCG Prescribing Lead, Hammersmith PCG

Dr Martin Murphy
Medical & Service Development Director, St Helens & Knowsley Health Authority

Melanie Ogden
Pharmaceutical Adviser, Manchester Health Authority

David Oxley
PCG Lead Pharmacist, Doncaster West PCG

Carol Palmer
PCG Pharmacist, Newport LHG

Keith Pearson
PCG Prescribing Adviser, Calderdale PCG

David Phizackerley
Pharmaceutical Adviser, West Sussex Health Authority

Dr Anthony Rathbone
Medical Adviser, Shropshire Health Authority

Liz Reid
Medicines Management Pharmacist, South Manchester PCT

Pauline Robinson
PCG Prescribing Adviser, Central Northumberland PCG

Mark Robinson
PCG Prescribing Manager, Croydon Central PCG

Gul Root
Pharmaceutical Adviser, East Surrey Health Authority

Alaister Rutherford
PCG Prescribing Adviser, Bristol South PCG

Eric Saunderson
PCG Clinical Governance Lead, Romford PCG

Andy Scott-Clarke
Pharmaceutical Adviser, Bromley Health Authority

Rasila Shah
PCG Pharmaceutical Adviser, Marylebone PCG

Kevin Smith
PCG Pharmaceutical Adviser, Herefordshire PCG

Dawn Solomon
PCG Pharmaceutical Adviser, Newcastle West PCG

Dr Gill Speak
PCG Prescribing Adviser, Rossendale PCG

Dr Jacqueline Spiby
Director of Public Health, Bromley Health Authority

Dr Morag Stern
Medical Adviser, Coventry Health Authority

Diane Strong
Community Nurse & Clinical Governance Lead, Bridgend
LHG

Dr Krishan Syal
Clinical Governance Lead, Blaenau Gwent LHG

Andy Taylor
PCG Prescribing Adviser, Bromsgrove District PCG

Sara Thomas
Pharmaceutical Adviser, Lechyd Morgannwg Health Authority

Angus Thompson
PCG Pharmaceutical Adviser, South Somerset PCG

Chris Thompson
Chief Pharmacist, Royal Devon & Exeter Healthcare NHS Trust

Professor David Upton
Chief Pharmacist, Glenfield Hospital, University Hospitals of Leicester NHS Trust

Anne Want
PCG Pharmacist, East Merton & Furzedown PCG

Helen Whiteside
Pharmaceutical Adviser, Leeds Health Authority

Dr Medwyn Williams
Clinical Governance Lead, Anglesey LHG

Karen Wynn
PCG Prescribing Adviser, Eastern Barnsley PCG

Other acknowledgements

In addition, the authors thank everyone who contributed to, and commented on, the various drafts during the production of this handbook.

Appendix 5
How this handbook was produced

The NPC co-ordinated the development of this handbook with funding supplied by NICE. A Steering Group was convened to direct the project and a managing editor was appointed.

Once a draft framework for the handbook had been agreed by the Steering Group, a series of three focus groups were held, in Bristol, Manchester and London. These generated a wide range of ideas for the content. Based on these ideas, a first draft was produced for discussion by the Steering Group.

Further focus groups were held, in Cardiff, London and Manchester, to receive detailed comments and further ideas based on the first draft. A draft was also put on the NICE and NPC web sites for a three-week period for open consultation. Comments received also informed the development of the final version.

NICE is associated with the NPC through a funding contract. The Institute considers the work of this organisation to be of value to the NHS in England and Wales and recommends that it be used to inform decisions on service organisation and delivery. The views expressed are those of the contributors and do not necessarily reflect the position of the Institute or the NPC.

Bibliography

A First Class Service: quality in the new NHS. Department of Health, 1998.

Area Prescribing Committees: maintaining effectiveness in the modern NHS. A guide to good practice. First Edition. National Prescribing Centre, September 2000.

Clinical Guidelines: using clinical guidelines to improve patient care within the NHS. NHS Executive, 1996.

Department of Health Letter to Chief Executives of Health Authorities – allocation of extra resources for 2000/01. 28.3.00.

Effective Health Care: getting evidence into practice. NHS Centre for Reviews and Dissemination. February 1999, Volume 5, Number 1.

Experience, Evidence and Everyday Practice: creating systems for delivering effective health care. Dunning M, *et al*. King's Fund, 1999.

The Front-Line Evidence-Based Medicine Project: Final Report. Donald, A. NHS Executive North Thames Regional Office R&D, 1998.

Getting Better with Evidence: experiences of putting evidence into practice. King's Fund and NHS Executive, 2000. http://www.doh.gov.uk/ntrd/getbtr.htm#2

GP Prescribing Support: a resource document and guide for the New NHS. NPC and NHS Executive, 1998.

Health Improvement Programmes: core guidance and framework documents. Issued with WHC (2000) 001. Health Service Strategy 1, National Assembly for Wales. 28 January 2000.

Health Improvement Programmes and Long-Term Agreements: guidance. WHC (1999) 087. 29 June 1999.

Implementing clinical practice guidelines: can guidelines be used to improve clinical practice? Effective Health Care 1(8). NHS Centre for Reviews and Dissemination, 1994.

Joint Priorities for Health and Social Services. Guidance from the National Assembly for Wales (in preparation).

Managing Antibiotic Resistance: a practical guide. NPC and Edgecumbe Health, 2000.

Modernising Health and Social Services: National Priorities Guidance 2000/01–2002/03. HSC 1999/242, LAC(99)38. 21 December 1999.

Planning for Health and Health Care: incorporating guidance for Health and Local Authorities on Health Improvement Programmes, Service and Financial Frameworks, Joint Investment Plans and Primary Care Investment Plans. HSC 1999/244, LAC(99)39. 21 December 1999.

Practical Clinical Governance in Primary Care: managing antibiotic prescribing: audit handbook. National Prescribing Centre, March 2000.

Primary Care Groups and Prescribing Data: using MIQUEST software. National Prescribing Centre Information Resource, September 1999.

PRODIGY: practical support for clinical governance. National Prescribing Centre Information Resource, September 1999.

Putting Patients First. NHS Wales, January 1998.

Abbreviations

CHC: Community Health Council
CHD: Coronary Heart Disease
CD ROM: Read-only CD
CHI: Commission for Health Improvement
DPH: Director of Public Health
eBNF: electronic British National Formulary
eDTB: electronic Drug and Therapeutics Bulletin
eMeReC: electronic Medicines Resource Centre bulletin (produced by the NPC)
eMIMS: electronic Monthly Index of Medical Specialities
GPRD: General Practice Research Database
HA: Health Authority
HImP/HIP: Health Improvement Programme
IM&T: Information Management & Technology
LHG: Local Health Group (Wales)
LDC: Local Dental Committee
LMC: Local Medical Committee
LNMC: Local Nursing & Midwifery Committee
LPC: Local Pharmaceutical Committee
MAAG: Medical Audit Advisory Group
NICE: National Institute for Clinical Excellence
NPC: National Prescribing Centre
NSF: National Service Framework
OWAM: Organisations With A Memory
PACT: Prescribing Analysis and CosT data
PALS: Patient Advocacy and Liaison Services
PAMS: Professions Allied to Medicine
PARC: Practice Audit Report and Catalogue

PCCAG: Primary Care Clinical Audit Group

PCG: Primary Care Group (England)

PCO: Primary Care Organisation

PCT: Primary Care Trust (England)

PMR: Patient Medication Record

PPI: Proton Pump Inhibitor (used in the management of dyspepsia)

PRIMIS: PRIMary Care Information System

PRODIGY: Prescribing RatiOnally with Decision support In General practice studY

RCN: Royal College of Nursing

RPSGB: Royal Pharmaceutical Society of Great Britain

SaFF: Service and Financial Framework (this may change to incorporate workforce planning)

Trust: Acute and community trusts

Index

abbreviations 137–8
action plans
  developing 14, 25–6, 59–67, 101–3
  publicising 14, 17–19, 33–4
Addenbrooke's NHS Trust 103
aids 47–89
aims, of handbook 1–3
approach, determining implementation
  62–3
audit
  guidance 14, 43–4
  methodologies 67
  practice changing 82
awareness, raising guidance 62

Barnet, Enfield & Haringey Health
  Authority 95
barriers
  to change 35–8, 39–41, 63
  to progress 39–41
baseline data, establishing 62
Bexley, Bromley & Greenwich Health
  Authority 101–2
bibliography 135–6
Birmingham Health Authority 93
Bro Morgannwg Trust 102–3

change
  barriers 35–8, 39–41, 63
  managing required 81–4
  sustaining 35–8

checklists 47–89
CHI see Commission for Health
  Improvement
circulating guidance 14, 33–4, 79,
  107–11
clinical audit see audit
clinical governance planning, and
  audits 43–4
clinical guidance, NICE guidance
  form 9
clinical practice
  identifying 61
  improving 82
clinical teams 61, 68
co-operation 17–19
co-ordinators, appointing 61
Commission for Health Improvement
  (CHI) 40, 119
computerised information systems 82–3
consulting widely 35–8
continuing professional development
  14, 81
customisation, guidance 80

data
  baseline, establishing 62
  sources, example 86
delegation
  NICE guidance responsibility 93–4
  workload 16
diagrammatic representation,
  implementation 49

dissemination
　changing practice　81
　options　79
　routes　9–10
duplication, avoiding　15–16

education
　importance　14
　monitoring　40
　needs　65
Effective Health Care Bulletin　36
evaluation, guidance　14, 43–4
examples, explained　1
expertise, additional　55

feedback
　implementation　14, 45–6
　mechanisms　45
　practice changing　82
　processes　67
　template　87
financial resources
　monitoring　40
　see also funding implications
focus, implementation　15–16
focus group members　123–8
forms of NICE guidance　9–11
funding implications　21–3
　see also financial resources

groups, NICE guidance implementation
　52–5
guidance directly received, organisations
　72–8

Hammersmith Hospitals NHS Trust
　93–4
handbook
　aims　1–3
　production　133
health authorities
　guidance directly received　72–3
　individuals and groups　52
　responsibilities　59
　see also named authorities

implementation
　action plans　14, 17–19, 25–6, 33–4,
　　59–67, 101–3
　approach　62–3
　audit　14, 43–4, 61, 66, 82
　circulating guidance　14, 33–4, 79,
　　107–11
　diagrammatic representation　49
　evaluation　14, 43–4
　feedback　14, 45–6, 67, 82, 87
　initiating　14, 17–19, 95–8
　local approach　14, 18, 29–31, 66, 79,
　　107–11
　mechanisms　64
　monitoring guidance　14, 39–41, 112
　networks　64
　personnel　14, 15–16, 22, 27–8, 52–5,
　　105–6
　practical tips　81–4
　resources　14, 21–3, 40, 58, 63, 99–100
　schematic　104
　steps　13–14, 69–70
　strategies　14, 35–8
individuals, NICE guidance
　implementation　52–5
information
　management　64
　sources　40
information systems, computerised
　82–3
information technology, using　65,
　82–3
initiating implementation　14, 17–19,
　95–8
intervention techniques, using　35–8
interventions, practice changing　81–4

Leeds Community and Mental Health
　Services NHS Trust　110
Leeds Teaching Hospitals NHS Trust
　107–9
Liverpool Health Authority　111
local approach, implementation　14, 18,
　29–31, 66, 79, 107–11

Manchester Health Authority   106
mechanisms
   feedback   45
   implementation   64
media campaigns, practice changing   83
members
   focus group   123–8
   steering groups   5–7
milestones
   action plans   25–6
   determining   64
   progress   39–41
monitoring
   guidance implementation   14, 39–41,
      112
   methods   66
   outcomes   39–41
   template   85

National Prescribing Centre
   (NPC)   117–18
networks, implementation   64
NHS Trusts
   guidance directly received   75–6
   individuals and groups   54
   responsibilities   59
NICE/NICE guidance, described
   115–16
nice.org.uk   9, 116
North & East Devon Health Authority
   99–100
Nottingham City Hospital NHS Trust
   111
NPC see National Prescribing Centre

organisations, guidance directly received
   72–8
outcomes, monitoring   39–41
Oxfordshire Health Authority   95–7

PCO see primary care organisation
personnel
   implementation   14, 15–16, 22, 27–8,
      52–5, 105–6
   resource implications   22

plans
   action   14, 17–19, 25–6, 33–4, 59–67,
      101–3
   clinical governance   43–4
   questions for implementation   56–7
   work   17–19
Plymouth Community Services Trust
   97–8
policy statement, priorities forum
   96–7
practical examples   91–112
practical tips, implementation   81–4
primary care organisations (PCOs)
   guidance directly received   74
   individuals and groups   53
   responsibilities   60
   terminology   10–11
PRIMIS/MIQUEST   40, 89
PRODIGY decision support tool   65,
   83, 89
production, of handbook   133
publicising
   action plans   14, 17–19, 33–4
   guidance implementation   66, 79
   results   45–6, 79

questions, implementation planning
   56–7

'recommendation proforma'   71
referral advice, NICE guidance form   9
reminders, practice changing   82
resources
   affected   58
   identifying   63
   implications   14, 21–3, 99–100
   monitoring   40
responsibilities
   delegating   93–4
   determining   59–60
   health authorities   59
   NHS Trusts   59
   PCOs   60
results, publicising   45–6, 79

Sefton Clinical Governance Forum 112

selecting, guidance elements 43–4

service delivery, monitoring 40

sources
  data, example 86
  information 40

staff, affected 58

stakeholders
  interests 67
  involving 25–6, 27–8, 35–8, 61–2

STAMP *see* Stockport Technologies And Managed Prescribing Forum

steering groups
  appointing 61
  members 5–7

steps, implementation 13–14, 69–70

Stockport Health Authority 105

Stockport Technologies And Managed Prescribing (STAMP) Forum 105

strategies, guidance 14, 35–8

success criteria, defining 63

teams, clinical teams 61, 68

technology appraisals, NICE guidance form 9

templates
  feedback 87
  monitoring 85

terminology 10–11

timescales
  action plans 25–6
  determining 64

timetable 17–19

tips, practical 81–4

training
  monitoring 40
  needs 65

websites, useful 88–9

Welsh language availability 9

work plans 17–19

work programme, NICE 50–1

workforce, monitoring 40

working groups, identifying 15–16